MILITANT WORKERS

Harry McShane at Baxter House Retirement Home, 1987 (Courtesy of the Glasgow Film and Video Workshop).

MILITANT WORKERS

LABOUR AND CLASS CONFLICT ON THE CLYDE, 1900–1950

Edited by
ROBERT DUNCAN
and
ARTHUR McIVOR

Essays in Honour of Harry McShane
1891–1988

JOHN DONALD PUBLISHERS LTD
EDINBURGH

ISBN 0 85976 373 0

British Library Cataloguing in Publication Data
A catalogue record for this book is available from the British Library

Phototypeset by The Midlands Book Typesetting Company, Loughborough
Printed and bound in Great Britain by J.W. Arrowsmith Ltd., Bristol

Contributors

Terry Brotherstone

Lecturer in History, University of Aberdeen; Amongst numerous publications, editor of *Covenant, Charter and Party* (1989) and a recently published anthology on Trotsky.

Raymond Challinor

Formerly Lecturer and Head of History Group, Newcastle Polytechnic; Amongst numerous publications, author of a biography of John S. Clarke, and *The Origins of British Bolshevism* (1977)

Robert Duncan

Tutor Organiser, Workers' Educational Association, West Scotland; Chair, Scottish Labour History Society; Amongst numerous publications, author of *Wishaw: Life and Labour in a Lanarkshire Community, 1790–1914* (1986); *Steelopolis: The Making of Motherwell, c. 1750–1939* (1991); co-editor of the *Warwick Guide to Labour Periodicals* (1977).

Glasgow Labour History Workshop

A research collective operating since 1986 and based in the History Department, University of Strathclyde. Authors of *The Singer Strike, Clydebank, 1911* (1989). The group involved in the 1910–14 project consisted of Ishbel Ballantyne, Louise Christie, Ricky Devlin, Billy Kenefick, Arthur McIvor, Hugh Paterson, Irene Sweeney and Liz Tuach.

Eric Heffer

Formerly Labour MP and government minister; colleague of Harry McShane; Amongst numerous publications, author of *Never a Yes Man* (Autobiography, 1991)

Arthur McIvor

Lecturer, Department of History, University of Strathclyde; Scottish Labour History Society Committee and Editorial Board member; Amongst numerous publications, co-editor of *Employers and Labour in the English Textile Industries, 1850–1939* (1988).

Hugh Paterson

Associate of Harry McShane; lifelong labour activist; retired history teacher recently completed M.Phil research on the Clyde seamen and their unions, c.1880–1914, at the University of Strathclyde.

George Rawlinson

Officer with Scottish Asian Action Committee; previously a part-time history tutor/lecturer at Salford University and Glasgow Polytechnic; M.Sc on the Incidence and Experience of Unemployment in Preston, 1929–1939.

Hugh Savage

Close associate of Harry McShane and lifelong labout activist; Co-author, with Les Forster, of *All for the Cause: Willie Nairn, 1956–1902* (1991)

James D. Young

A former Reader in History, now a Senior Fellow at the University of Stirling; A Fellow of the Royal Historical Society and lifelong socialist; author of numerous books and articles on labour history, including *The Rousing of the Scottish Working Class* (1979); *Socialism and the English Working Class* (1989); *John Maclean: Clydeside Socialist 1879–1923* (1992)

Acknowledgements

In preparing this collection of essays we have accumulated many debts which we would like to duly acknowledge. Our first and foremost debt is to the late Harry McShane, to whom this book is dedicated. Two of Harry's close associates, Hugh Savage and Les Forster, provided much encouragement, some illustrations and invaluable aid with details of Harry's life. Special thanks are also due to Audrey Canning at the Gallacher Memorial Library for help with sources and for searching out rare pamphlets written by Harry. We are also obliged for financial and secretarial assistance from numerous institutional sponsors, notably the Scottish Labour History Society; the History Department, University of Strathclyde; WEA, West Scotland; the Scottish Trades Union Congress; John Maclean Society; Midlothian Trades Council; Paisley Trades Council; UCATT (Dalkeith). We would also like to thank all those persons, too numerous to mention individually, who contributed to our appeal for funds to help subsidise this publication. Finally, many thanks to Margaret Hastie and Alison Armour for word processing the lion's share of the manuscript.

Glasgow, 1992   R.D.
                                                         A.McI.

Note

The front cover illustration shows Harry McShane (with cap in centre) leading the Glasgow to London hunger march, January 1934 (From John McGovern: *Neither Fear nor Favour*, 1960).

Contents

CHAPTER 1
Introduction

Rob Duncan and Arthur McIvor

This book arose from a suggestion made by Hugh Savage and Les Forster that the Scottish Labour History Society might organise some form of memorial to Harry McShane, one of the last of the 'Red Clydesiders' who died on 13 April 1988, aged 96. This proposal was taken through the Glasgow Labour History Workshop to the SLHS executive committee who were extremely receptive towards the idea. The Society agreed to arrange an edited collection of essays as an appropriate tribute to Harry's memory. We both accepted the task of coordinating the compilation, launching an appeal for sponsorship, commissioning chapters and editing the text. From the outset we aimed to bring together a cluster of essays, based largely on original historical research, which dealt with aspects of Harry's experience or with issues close to Harry's heart. The core theme is Clydeside labour and militancy during the first half of the twentieth century – a period when, according to one commentator, Glasgow represented the 'Red Capital' of the British Empire. We have also incorporated a few short reminiscences of Harry and a sample of his own political writing. This book thus provides a very modest companion volume to the rich and detailed autobiography by Harry McShane and Joan Smith, *No Mean Fighter*, published by Pluto Press in 1978.

Harry McShane had quite an unusual political pedigree. He was born in May 1891 in Glasgow. His background was Irish catholic and both his father and grandfather were building labourers. Harry was apprenticed to engineering, starting work in Howden's, Glasgow, in 1907. His formative education took place on Glasgow Green before World War One, where he learned to argue and reason, debating religion and politics. The deep recession of 1908–9 and the ensuing unemployment relief campaign in Glasgow helped to convert him to socialism. He joined the Independent Labour Party in August 1909 and around the same time, much influenced by Robert Blatchford's atheistic literature, broke with catholicism. Harry quickly became disillusioned with what he regarded as the sterile parliamentary socialism of the ILP. After two years he left to affiliate to the newly formed British Socialist Party, influenced by the enigmatic Victor Grayson. By 1910–11, Harry was already a committed revolutionary Marxist. He became firmly implanted within the anti-war strand of the BSP, which opposed Hyndman's rabidly jingoistic stance during World War One. He joined the armed forces in 1915 to spread socialist propaganda, but, finding the volunteer army impenetrable, deserted and returned to Glasgow, from where he was forced to go to sea for a while to avoid police detection.

After the war, in 1920, Harry left the BSP and joined forces with John Maclean in a small propagandist organisation known as Tramp Trust Unlimited. This group operated closest to the Socialist Labour Party and during this period Harry wrote extensively for the SLP paper, *The Socialist*. With the onset of severe economic depression during the winter of 1920–21 he started campaigning and organising on behalf of the unemployed, a task he described as his 'chief work as a revolutionary'. After the Tramp Trust dissolved he broke with John Maclean and joined the fledgling Communist Party of Great Britain in 1922, partly because of its active work in organising the unemployed. He stayed within the CP until 1953. Thereafter, whilst he remained politically active, he eschewed any formal links with political parties.

Harry McShane was a member of the Amalgamated Society of Engineers (later AUEW) and, when in charge of the Scottish edition of the *Daily Worker*, the National Union of Journalists. He laid great stress on the importance of industrial organisation, on fostering self-activity in the workplace and workers' control over production. He became an advocate of syndicalist ideas, influenced significantly by Willie Gallacher and Tom Mann before and during World War One. He always stressed the

The Tramp Trust Unlimited, *c.* 1920–21; Right to left: Harry McShane, James D. MacDougall, John Maclean, Sandy Ross, Peter Marshall (Courtesy of The National Library of Scotland).

importance of political and industrial activity, though personally he was always more active as a propagandist and organiser within his political branch than his trade union. He was, however, a shop steward in Weir's just prior to the First World War, was involved in several strikes (including the 1919 forty hours' strike) and came into direct contact during the War with the Clyde Workers' Committee, though he was not a leading member. Harry argued that the 1908–9 unemployment agitation followed by the labour unrest of 1910–14 radically altered the socialist movement. In Chapter 4, the dimensions and causes of this pre-war phase of labour unrest on Clydeside are examined in some detail by the Glasgow Labour History Workshop. They argue that a whole series of alienating factors coagulated to stimulate a strike wave of unprecedented proportions, that this militancy was sustained right up to World War One and that culmulatively this represented the beginnings of a sustained challenge to capitalist hegemony on the Clyde which was to reach fruition during the War and immediate post-war period, 1915–20.

Recently, the whole issue of 'Red Clydeside' in which Harry McShane's life was inextricably enmeshed has generated a most intense debate amongst historians. The rather exaggerated and romanticised notions of a revolutionary upsurge on Clydeside after World War One, promulgated particularly in Willie Gallacher's autobiography, *Revolt on the Clyde* (1936), have now been firmly refuted. However, the discourse over the nature of class conflict and social relations on the Clyde over the pivotal period from the outbreak of World War One to the mid-1920s continues to attract the attention of historians. In Chapter 3, Terry Brotherstone critically reviews the tangled twists and turns of the 'Red Clydeside' debate, contending that the debunking exercise of Iain McLean, Christopher Harvie and others in the early 1980s has now been effectively neutralised. He argues for a renewed investigation of the 'Red Clydeside' phenomenon which builds on recent interpretations of the effective political networking activities which were particularly associated with the Independent Labour Party between 1915 and the early 1920s. Brotherstone goes on to make a case for a re-opening of the historical and political debate on the significance of the formation and nature of the Communist Party of Great Britain, revolutionary internationalist perspectives and an assault on notions of 'British exceptionalism' in analyses of past and contemporary class struggle.

In Chapter 5, Rob Duncan explores the movement for independent working-class education and the germination of the Labour College movement in West Scotland. Harry McShane was a great orator, propagandist, pamphleteer and political journalist, renowned for his grasp of Marxist thought and his debating skills. He always stressed the importance of applied learning, was one of the widest read individuals within the labour movement and advocated, indeed personified, a synthesis of theory and practice. Through the Tramp Trust, Harry was directly involved in workers' education and supported the concept of a Scottish Labour College in which his colleague John Maclean was a leading figure. Duncan contends that the emergent movement for 'independent working-class education' was an integral part of a confident labour and socialist challenge to 'capitalist civilisation', and represented an important episode in a wider socialist counter-culture which has yet to be fully investigated in the context of early twentieth-century Glasgow and the West of Scotland.

The struggle in Ireland was always a key issue within the Scottish labour movement and a theme that Harry campaigned upon time and time again. Most Scottish socialists supported Home Rule for Ireland and James Connolly's books were widely read. Harry agitated actively on Clydeside in support of Jim Larkin during the Irish transport workers' strike in Dublin in 1913 and, later, the Tramp Trust were amongst the few left political groups actively to support the struggle of the Irish Republican Army for independence from British rule over 1920–21. Much later still, after the developments in Northern Ireland in 1968–9, Harry took up the Irish issue again and spoke at numerous meetings in favour of a united Ireland, with equal political and employment rights for all religious factions. In Chapter 7, Jim Young explores the links between Clydeside socialism and the Easter Rising of 1916. Alongside an interpretation of the political standpoints of three key figures, and of the perceptions of American-Irish socialism, Young asserts that the British left either did not understand, or were generally hostile to the Easter Rising. Only later, Young postulates, with the growth of revolutionary socialism within Irish labour from 1918 and subsequent British imperialist atrocities did a more radicalised Clydeside socialism become more receptive to the Irish republican cause.

Harry McShane's reputation within the British labour movement was really earned through his involvement with the unemployed workers' movement between the wars. He became the most dynamic organiser of unemployed demonstrations in Scotland in the early 1920s and, after a spell working in England and Alaska, returned to this work in 1930. He became Glasgow district secretary and Scottish organiser for the National Unemployed Workers' Movement, responsible for organising hunger marches to Edinburgh, and the Scottish contingent on the national hunger marches to London in 1932 and 1934. He and Wal Hannington were great friends during this period of tireless activity on behalf of the unemployed. In chapter 8, George Rawlinson examines the work of the NUWM in three areas of West Scotland during this phase of most intensive activity during the early 1930s. He emphasises the broad base of the movement, the shoddy treatment of the NUWM by the official labour and trade union movement and the successes achieved through agitation and mass action on the streets which effectively mobilised working-class communities to fight against the obscenity of unemployment and the degradation of the Means Test.

Socialists, communists and others within the revolutionary left made enormous personal sacrifices for their political beliefs in the first half of the twentieth century. The integrity and raw courage of many socialists of this period is difficult to exaggerate. Discrimination and victimisation were rife – sackings remained common on Clydeside even for union and strike activity before World War Two. For this reason, some activists adopted the use of an alias to obtain work. Police spies honeycombed the labour movement. Socialists, as Harry McShane noted, were invariably regarded as criminal deviants and treated severely by the law. CPers charged with criminal libel, for example, were commonly sent down for 2–3 years in the 1930s. Harry had first-hand experience of such tactics on numerous occasions. He was sacked from Howden's because he refused to blackleg and from A.W. Smiths in May 1920 after his foreman saw him chairing a meeting for John Maclean. In Chapter 6, McIvor and Paterson examine the evolving networks of victimisation and political discrimination on Clydeside up to World War Two and consider the implications of such tactics, which represented a serious breach of civil liberties. Special attention is paid to the anti-labour propaganda activities and political blacklisting role of the Economic League.

After the NUWM was disbanded during World War Two Harry McShane became Scottish Organiser of the *Daily Worker* (Scottish edition) and threw his energies into political journalism. Two issues dominated. During the war, the campaign to open a second front. Immediately after the war, housing shortages were the key issue for Harry. This brought him into conflict with the Glasgow Town Council and some heated exchanges with the housing committee. In this period in the mid–late 1940s Harry wrote four pamphlets on housing, each of which sold over 10,000 copies, distributed primarily door-to-door by the CP. Two of these pamphlets, produced over 1946–7, dealing with conditions in Glasgow and, particularly, the Gorbals, are reproduced in Chapter 2. Such conditions were exposed by Harry with the object of stimulating housebuilding, especially the construction of temporary accommodation to solve this post-war housing crisis.

Harry McShane endorsed the worst excesses of Stalinism from the 1930s through his membership of the Communist Party of Great Britain. However, he was one of the most independent thinkers within the CPGB and fought and defied the official party line on many occasions (for example, the free speech fight in 1931, the Edinburgh hunger march in 1933 and over the issue of Stalinist branch education classes, which Harry refused to introduce in the Gorbals). Harry found the Lenin and Stalin hero-worship aspects of the party obnoxious. He despaired at the lack of debate within the party and resented the dogmatism of the Moscow-school CPers, especially Peter Kerrigan. His unorthodox, dissident stance was made possible by his standing within the National Unemployed Workers' Movement, the CP's only mass organisation, and his power base within the Gorbals CP branch. His disagreements with the party line intensified in the late 1940s and early 1950s, as the CP reorientated its strategy towards cooperation with the Labour Party, commitment to central planning and the peaceful, parliamentary route to socialism, thus eschewing commitment to revolutionary class struggle. In Harry's mind, this represented a radical and misguided shift from Marxist ideas. Hugh Savage and Ray Challinor refer to these developments in their contributions within Chapter 1. Characteristically, Harry fought these reformist tendencies from within and was increasingly marginalised within the CP because of his heretical views. For two years before he broke with the party the Glasgow

CP Committee failed to invite Harry to speak to any meetings and attempted, unsuccessfully, to remove him from his position as Gorbals secretary. He resigned from the CP in 1953 after being given an ultimatum to change his attitude or face expulsion.

Harry's activity within the labour movement continued after 1953, though he later admitted that he felt isolated from mass activity outwith the CP. Initially, he attempted, with Eric Heffer, to form a loose federation of Marxist groups. They successfully sustained a new journal, *Revolt*, for almost two years. Eric Heffer's contribution to chapter 1, written in January 1990, fills in some of the background of these developments (*Note*: a fuller account appeared subsequently in his autobiography, *Never a Yes Man*, published shortly after his death in 1991). From the late 1950s, Harry became a Marxist-Humanist, linking himself with a group of American theorists whose leading figure was Raya Dunayevskaya. He returned to working with the tools, in Harland and Wolff's shipyard, became chairman of his AUEW branch and was elected as a delegate to the Glasgow Trades Council. He became actively involved in campaigns within the GTC, including anti-nuclear demonstrations and the campaign to save shipbuilding jobs in the 1960s. In his mid-80s he was active in the Right to Work campaign, joining the march and speaking at the Albert Hall in 1976. He also read and wrote extensively, and spoke frequently on public platforms on Marxist theory, current issues and the history of the labour movement (including Glasgow May Day rallies right up to the mid-1980s). He was at his happiest in the cut and thrust of debate. On one celebrated occasion he earned the (somewhat dubious) praise of Jim Callaghan and Dennis Healy for the way in which he completely destroyed the arguments of the Tory Education minister, Lord Boyle, during the bicentenary conference at the Adam Smith Institute in 1976.

Harry McShane believed passionately in the self-organisation of ordinary workers and rejected the crude reductionist version of Marxism which emphasised that human agency was at the mercy of wider economic forces. He was an organic intellectual of his class in the truest sense of the term, and right up to his death he remained optimistic about the revolutionary potential of the working class. One of his obituarists, William Hunter, quite appropriately, dubbed him 'the humane Marxist' (*Glasgow Herald*, 14 April 1988). We hope that this modest collection of essays, focusing on a few topics that intersect with Harry McShane's long life will serve as a tribute to a man whose tireless activism on behalf of ordinary working people provides inspiration to the present and coming generation of socialists.

Remembering Harry
(i). Harry McShane: Some Personal Recollections
Hugh Savage

The first time I had any personal contact with Harry McShane was when the Glasgow city committee of the Communist Party made me election agent for Peter Kerrigan in the Gorbals by-election of 1948. As a good little Stalinist, I did as I was told. I was viewed with suspicion by the Gorbals CP members. I remember after my first meeting of the election committee leaving the premises with Bob Saunders, who was the district organiser of the Plumbing Trades Union. Harry McShane closed the door after us and as he did so he asked us where we stayed (Harry at this time had a room in the Gorbals branch premises). Quite cheerily, I said, 'Oh, we go east'. Harry replied, 'That is quite appropriate, all the wise men come from the east'. I have no doubt that as I had a long experience as group leader in the CP factory branch in John Brown's; was active in the Bridgeton branch of the CP; and also had formed a Housing Association in Bridgeton, this gave me the tough pedigree that could face up to McShane and the rebellious members of the Gorbals branch. As I started organising and working with Harry and the Gorbals comrades I came to realise that the cynicism with which they greeted some of the decisions of the Glasgow Committee was not entirely misplaced. I found to my surprise that there were sound political differences, which I will deal with later.

As the date of the by-election was announced, it became necessary for me to give up my job in Fairfields' shipyard, where I worked as a plumber's welder, and become a full-time agent for the period of the election campaign. As I was also a shop steward in the yard I knew there would be no way I could return. As I was married with a young family I assumed that I would receive the normal wages a party organiser got. However, to my surprise Bob McIlhone, the Glasgow secretary, gave me at least £5 a week more. I felt uncomfortable about it and sought Harry's advice. He told me not to take any hand-outs; get the rate for the job and no more. I returned the extra cash.

The election campaign was really outstanding. For a while it looked as if Kerrigan could break the mould and be successful. But we reckoned without the silent majority and the Catholic vote. However, the 8,000 that the CP polled was the best vote for a communist candidate in Scotland. The Labour candidate was Alice Cullen, who had been a councillor for 11 years in the Glasgow Corporation. She was not at the races. With over a thousand activists from the CP and the Young Communist League we really set the Gorbals alight. Unfortunately, we didn't quite get enough votes! There were also several disquieting features of the election campaign that were not apparent to most comrades involved. Peter Kerrigan was an imposing looking candidate standing over six feet tall, with grey distinguished hair, a fit man – ex-Junior soccer player with Yoker Athletic. However, he was also quite an aloof person, who tended to lecture to people rather than talk to them. I never got on friendly terms with him in the eight weeks or so of the election. He was a man who never strayed from the party line. In the election committee meetings his contribution was completely unimaginative and quite predictable, whereas Harry McShane's proposals and comments were usually different and invariably original. This was no doubt to be expected, given his long record of activity in the labour movement, his position as Scottish correspondent of the *Daily Worker* and chairman of the Glasgow branch of the National Union of Journalists. Harry's access to most newspapers and the media got Peter Kerrigan actively involved in issues that none of the other candidates knew about. It was Harry who gave Alice Cullen the title of 'silent Alice'. He knew she had been on the Glasgow Corporation for eleven years and had never spoken once at a Corporation meeting.

So, I was flabbergasted two weeks into the campaign when I got a telephone call from John Gollan to the Gorbals rooms

Communist Party Election Rooms, Crown St, Gorbals in 1948. Harry McShane is on the back row, with spectacles; Hugh Savage on the front row holding a book (Courtesy of Hugh Savage).

telling me that he was sending up Malcolm McEwen to relieve Harry McShane from the job as press secretary for the election. He told me to tell Peter Kerrigan, but not to tell Harry. This I could not do. I immediately told Harry and then told Kerrigan. I had absolutely no quarrel with Malcolm McEwen, who was a very capable journalist, having been a feature writer for the *Daily Worker*. This was my first but not my last experience of double-dealing within the Communist Party.

This was the beginning of a close relationship with Harry McShane that lasted for forty years. The next battles took place in the CP's Glasgow city committee, where we were both regarded as deviationists. In actual fact all we wanted was for the party to get actively involved in all struggles, whether official or unofficial. On one occasion we were accused of being adventurers because Les Forster suggested during a campaign that we should throw a few thousand leaflets out of the top windows of Lewis's store into Argyle Street. Another issue that created divisions was housing. While the full-time officials of the CP did not openly condemn the comrades who, in order to spotlight the dire shortage of houses (the council house waiting list was nearly 100,000) had started to assist people in insanitary houses to withhold their rents, their support was only lukewarm. At this period there were many thousands of empty houses in private hands which those of us involved in the struggle for homes saw as places to be utilised to rehouse the homeless. This led to the squatters' movement which to begin with was entirely spontaneous, but a few comrades like Les Forster and John Gold from Bridgeton were to the fore. It is significant that the only leading communist who was involved with them, particularly helping with publicity and legal aid, was Harry McShane.

Another small issue that came up over this period was the question of misrepresentation. Two leading officials in the CP got posters printed saying that they were 'Housing Candidates' in the municipal election. There was no mention of their party membership or the fact that they were full-time officials. Harry regarded this as deception and had the posters destroyed. In his opinion this was one indication of the growing desire for respectability within the movement. Harry believed strongly in declaring your communist principles and joining the workers in struggle.

In his autobiography, *No Mean Fighter*, Harry mentions a few events that led to him leaving the Communist Party. He was set against paid officials who only liked discussion within the party on the line that had been laid down from the Central Committee. They tended to dictate policy and direct any action through official channels, frowning more and more upon small, unofficial strikes. In contrast, those Party members who left the CP for purely selfish reasons, either to join the Labour Party or to become a full-time official in a trade union still seemed to be acceptable to the Party leaders. Many of these people, even those who became MPs, were still regarded as CP allies, despite the fact that, in thought and action, they were real right wingers. I remember Harry telling me about a meeting of the Comintern in Moscow in the 1920s when the British delegation – including the two Scottish delegates – took a particular decision on the role of the CPGB within Britain. The meeting then adjourned for lunch. However, when they returned, to Harry's surprise, the previous decision was dropped and the exact opposite was put forward. Finlay Hart, the other Scottish delegate, went along with the change, but Harry did not. Harry was always suspicious of unanimous decisions and was not afraid of disagreements and discussion, provided they led to action. I feel this was one of the reasons he was respected within the labour movement. Finlay Hart, incidentally, was the only prominent member of the CP to be present at Harry's funeral.

The one question consistently raised when Harry spoke at meetings was 'why did you leave the CP?' As a matter of fact, one of the last meetings he spoke at was one organised by the Glasgow Labour History Workshop at Strathclyde University, on the theme of the Russian Revolution. As usual, the same question was raised; 34 years after he left the party it still came up. His answer was straightforward. He argued that the CP was no longer a revolutionary party and the Soviet Union was not and never had been a socialist country. Long before Dubchek called for 'communism with a human face', Harry had turned to Marxist Humanism. He did not require the Hungarian tragedy to resign from the CP. When the Hungarian uprising did occur, Harry immediately supported it. In answer to the Soviet allegations about Fascists and the involvement of the CIA he commented along these lines: 'When do you ever see Fascists setting up workers' councils?'.

Harry McShane remained within the Communist Party for over 30 years. However, his influence within the party was not all that significant, particularly with the new leaders who had attended the Lenin school in Moscow. His conversion to Marxism had taken a very different route. He was self-taught and one of the best-read people in the socialist movement. He always returned to Marxism and never tired of explaining its importance to young people. One of his favourite stories was how Marx took Pierre Proudhon's *Philosophy of Poverty* and showed (by turning Proudhon on his head when he wrote *The Poverty of Philosophy*) how it was the emerging working class with their labour power for sale that were the 'gravediggers' of capitalism, not the petty bourgeoisie. Harry had a great deal of respect for the Scottish philosophers like Adam Ferguson and Adam Smith. He relished the fact that whilst Marx rejected many of their conclusions, he paid tribute to the contribution they made to the development of philosophical theory.

Harry McShane was indeed the last of the 'Red Clydesiders'. He never lost his fundamental belief in the socialist cause. He had many offers to join other political parties – from the Labour Party to most of the left-wing parties. However, he was suspicious of their rigidity, and, after his experiences in the CP, had some doubts about the role of a vanguard party. He was no armchair philosopher and it always gladdened his heart when the workers won a victory as a result of strike action. While Harry had access to many establishment figures in Scotland, he never used this for personal advancement. He was completely and utterly incorruptible. He never sought any honours, although after some persuasion he did accept the award of Freeman of the City of Glasgow. After this was presented by the Lord Provost and the Glasgow Cathedral minister the band struck up 'I Belong to Glasgow', instead of the usual national anthem, much to the annoyance of the minister. When one looks at the Labour Lords, and at the people who have exploited the labour movement for personal gain, I almost always think about Harry McShane. A few days before he died I asked him how he was for money. He said 'I'm fine. I've got over £40'. Let that be his epitaph after 80 years as a Marxist.

CHAPTER 2

(ii). *Harry McShane and the Communist Party*

Ray Challinor

A comrade of John Maclean, prominent in those stormy days
that became known as 'the revolt on the Clyde', as well as
co-leader, along with Wal Hannington, of the Hunger Marches,
Harry McShane would have been remembered in working-class
history had he died before 1953. His real greatness, however,
came after 1953, when he resigned from the Communist Party.
Who would have thought that a person, already 62 years of
age, would still have 35 years of political activity in front of
him? It was in this last period that he made his distinctive
contribution.

His rupture with the CP was a courageous decision. Instead of
remaining a full time CP employee, with the prospect of a secure
– if not over-lavishly provided for – retirement, it meant he had
again to find employment in the shipyards. There he laboured
until he was 69 years old, a necessity if he were to qualify for
an old-age pension.

But Harry McShane's decision involved much more than this.
By taking it, he consigned himself to the outer darkness of
politics, inhabited only by a few lunatics who called themselves
revolutionary socialists. They were completely devoid of any
influence. In those days, the Labour and Communist Parties
bestrode the political world like two colossi. Almost everyone
on the left owed allegiance to one or the other.

In his 1935 diaries, Trotsky says that one of the great surprises
in a person's life is the sudden recognition of old age. In
other words, slowly and imperceptibly changes are taking place
and, then, suddenly there comes the awareness, the shock of

recognition, that what previously was accomplished with ease has now become an impossibility. The same process, I think, can happen to political parties. Because of its snail-like pace, often the transformation goes unrecorded and undetected.

It takes a considerable effort today, particularly for young people, to imagine the political magnetism that Labourism possessed in that post-war period. The Attlee government had introduced the welfare state, giving to every citizen, as of right, security from the cradle to the grave. Full employment had become a reality. It had provided a comprehensive National Health Service, where the criterion was need, not the ability to pay. Since then, no Labour programme has envisaged making such sweeping changes. Admittedly, the 1951 general election had been a setback, temporarily halting the march of social progress. Virtually nobody doubted, however, that progress towards the New Jerusalem would shortly be resumed.

Even in defeat, Labourism displayed a strength that has now long since departed. At the 1951 general election, it polled a record unprecedented 13.5 million votes. Since then, an extra 7 million people have been added to the electoral register. In part, this happened because of a lowering of the voting age from 21 to 18 years, a move that surely would aid any party appealing to the rebellious young. Yet, in the 1983 general election, Labour polled a post-war low – only 8.5 million votes. The figures themselves disguise the extent to which traditional Labour support had been eroded. They fail to take account of the fact that almost two million coloured immigrants have come to Britain since 1951 and most of them voted Labour. Moreover, if the decline of Labour's electoral strength has been lamentable, the falling number of party activists has been nothing short of disastrous. From a peak of 1.5 million in 1954, individual membership now hovers around the 300,000 mark.

So the party that Harry McShane turned his back on in 1953 was much bigger, more attractive and of far greater consequence than Labour is today. And the same goes for the Communist Party. It, too, felt it had history on its side. At the 1950 general election, the CP fielded 100 candidates. Amongst them was Harry Pollitt, the CP general secretary. Standing at Rhondda

East, he secured 4,463 votes, knocking the Conservatives into third place. Nevertheless, Pollitt conceded, after the result had been announced, that it had been a serious defeat. He consoled his supporters, however, by telling them that it had to be set alongside the tremendous triumph which communism had achieved in China. Its 700 million people had joined the communist camp, which stretched in monolithic unity from the Baltic sea to the Pacific ocean.

Communist confidence was further boosted by the conviction that the East had an economic system without inner contradictions, not afflicted by booms or slumps. Therefore, the Soviet Union had the capacity to make smooth and unimpeded industrial progress. In a climate of peaceful co-existence, the USSR would reveal in practice its superiority to the USA: communism would ultimately bury capitalism. By 1980, as Khrushchev informed the world, the standard of living in the Soviet Union would outstrip America's.

With Stalinism and Labourism, at least on the surface appearing to be so enticing, what caused Harry McShane to reject them in 1953, ploughing instead his own solitary political furrow? Three important principles, I think, guided him: First, his belief in socialist humanism, a corpus of ideas that had been developed by Raya Dunayevskaya in America. This gave him the conviction that man should be the measure of all things. Second, his view that America and Russia, whatever their superficial differences, fundamentally had the same social system. Both were run in the interests of the rich and powerful. In neither did working people have control of their lives. Rather, they were exploited and manipulated, treated as a mere cog in a wheel, where the over-riding need was increased production. Third, this situation, he thought, would provoke the masses to revolt, whether against Eastern state capitalism, or Western monopoly capitalism. For that reason, as he had done in his time with John Maclean, he did not struggle for influence in any party machine. His concern lay in aligning himself with, and helping to encourage, 'the new passions, the new forces' that came bubbling up from the lower depths of society.

Interestingly, Peter Petrov, another of John Maclean's old comrades, had a very similar approach. After participating in the class struggles on Clydeside, he returned to his native Russia. There he held numerous positions in the Soviet government, including belonging to the delegation that negotiated the Treaty of Brest-Litovsk. Emerging disagreements with Stalin, however, forced him to move first to Germany and then, as Hitler came to power, to flee to this country.

Here, in 1934, Petrov wrote a much neglected book, *The Secret of Hitler's Victory*. In it, he exposed the German Social Democratic and Communist parties. Both contributed to Hitler's final success: 'The masses vigorously demanded a united front. But the two bureaucratic party machines were united only in the rejection of a united front.' (p. 83). The Social Democrats, 'timid and uncertain in the face of the masses, would like to put off the socialist commonwealth into another world beyond the grave', whilst the communists, on the other hand, 'failed to take their own revolutionary socialist phrases seriously, and they acted merely as agents of the Russian state interests.' (p. 61). In conclusion, the book argued that the Soviet Union was state capitalist, having the same relationship with the working class as individual capitalists do elsewhere.

Though in essence, Petrov and Harry McShane shared the same views, a vital difference still remains. Not having a positive response to his book, Petrov became disillusioned with revolutionary socialism. Dying in 1947, politically his death had occurred many years before. By contrast, Harry McShane was not afraid to stand alone. Despite not having any organisational or financial backing, for 34 years he unselfishly devoted himself to the cause. The drudgery of typing, duplicating, collating and posting his *Marxist Humanist* was accomplished without complaint. Likewise, whether tired or ill, he would never refuse to address a meeting. It is in this selfless devotion that Harry's greatness lies.

CHAPTER 2

(iii). *Harry McShane and the Socialist Workers' Federation*
Eric S. Heffer

I believe I first saw Harry McShane when I was in the RAF and briefly stationed in Glasgow during the Second World War. It was at the time when the Communist International was shut down by Stalin. I was very concerned and visited Peter Kerrigan and his wife Rose, who lived in Pollokshaws, to discuss the situation. I wanted to know when the constituent parties had discussed the situation, and which of them had agreed to it. It seemed to me to be against the principle of working-class solidarity and internationalism. The answers I received to my questions were extremely unhelpful and I continued to have serious doubts. I also remember marching in uniform at the May Day demonstration which assembled at the City Chambers under the CP banner, and it was there that I am sure Harry McShane was first pointed out to me. I did not speak to him. However, I had read a pamphlet by him about John Maclean. Harry had been closely associated with John and had been one of his lieutenants in the so-called 'Tramp Trust'. This was a group of socialists who travelled and spoke all over Scotland, putting across the socialist message. I did not personally meet Harry until after he had left the CP, and his job as the *Daily Worker* correspondent in Scotland. I wrote to him indicating that I agreed with his public statement and he came down to Liverpool and stayed a few days at my house in Avondale Road.

I had been expelled from the CP in 1948 and after a period in the wilderness rejoined the Labour Party. However, I was not very happy with the way the Labour Party was going and felt that it was time to consider creating a new socialist party that

20

was neither Stalinist nor Social-Democratic. Harry left the CP with a number of younger colleagues, and they formed the Clyde Socialist Action Group. On Merseyside a number of us had got together and we had formed the Socialist Educational Group. Those who had left the CP with Harry were Eddie Donaldson, Les Forster, Alex Bernstein, Bill Gunn, Bill McCulloch, Hugh Savage and Matt McGinn. They were the basis of the Glasgow group. In Liverpool, there were comrades like I.P. Hughes, Neil Beresford, R.G. Bale and S. Sheldon. When Harry came to stay with us in Liverpool, naturally we discussed the political situation and what we thought should be done. We agreed that efforts should be made to get the various groups together and that we should organise a conference to this end in Liverpool. This was ultimately held on 17–18 July 1954. The conference heard a report from myself, based upon a lengthy resolution, and Harry took the chair. Before the conference, on 1 May 1954, the Clyde and Liverpool groups had issued a newspaper entitled *Revolt*, the price was 2d and it consisted of four pages. The first page leading article was written by Harry and was called 'Our Aims'. Harry analysed each of the main political parties on the Left. He said of the Labour Party: 'The Labour Party is a class struggle party, but the leaders deny the class struggle. It was built on the principle of working class solidarity but not with a socialist aim. MacDonald went over to the Tories, but his influence is still felt in Labour Party circles. The Labour Party cannot be ignored by Marxists because of its class basis and because it is the only immediate alternative to the Tories'. With regard to the CP he wrote: 'The Communist Party, never very strong, has dropped in prestige. It has wobbled in recent years on the class struggle. . .'. Because of these blunders it could not afford to allow criticism. Critics were either isolated or expelled. Conceit and arrogance took the place of political understanding with some of the jumped-up 'leaders' brought forward during and after the war. Applause counted with them, far more than activity of a mass character.

Harry did not spare the Trotskyists from his criticism. Of the Trotskyists (no doubt meaning all the 'orthodox' groups) he said: 'The Trotskyists are endeavouring to impose a tailor-made party on the British workers. It is to resemble the Communist Party of the Soviet Union when Trotsky was a leading member. It would be more narrow and doctrinaire than the CP in its early days. . . . Their appeal can never meet with success among the British workers.' Harry ended his article by saying: 'There is an urgent need for a new militant party of the workers, but that must come from the movement itself . . . We can prepare for it by spreading socialist principles. Our outlook must be revolutionary and our attitude to the opportunists must be uncompromising.'

The Liverpool conference set up the Federation of Marxist Groups and *Revolt* became the paper of the Federation. Later, the Federation became the Socialist Workers' Federation. One of its earliest campaigns was against conscription, in cooperation with the Independent Labour Party. In Glasgow, the Clyde branch of the SWF organised a series of John Maclean memorial lectures in the Central Halls, Bath Street, in November 1955, with Harry McShane as the lecturer, tackling such subjects as 'Class Struggle and Revolution' and 'John Maclean – Revolutionary Socialist'. Harry wrote regularly for *Revolt*. He was, after all, the national chairman from the beginning to the end of the organisation. In one article entitled 'The Last Fight' he commented: 'We will make greater progress if we get rid of the idea that the conquest of power by the working class is a long way off. Opportunism has seized hold of the Parliamentary Labour Party. . . . They do not reflect working class opinions. The workers will desert them in time.' Harry wrote articles about the need to fight conscription and other pieces explaining that the class war was a reality. All that he wrote and spoke about clearly had an impact on those who read him or heard him speak.

The SWF, although it gathered groups in London, Surrey, Liverpool and Glasgow, and had individual members elsewhere, never became a large organisation. It was quickly beset with internal arguments, especially from amongst the groups in London. Some of these were very sectarian in character and seemed to argue over dots and commas in the various statements that were formulated, discussed and issued. In fact the very thing that we tried to avoid was to some extent pushed upon to us.

We did, however, make some interesting contacts abroad. In Italy, we made contact with a group, mainly based in Milan, called 'Azione Communista'. They too had their sectarian squabbles and eventually split up, with a number of them becoming active in the Italian Socialist Party. The SWF also made contact with André Marty, the veteran French CP leader, who had been expelled from the CP and had written a book, *The Marty Affair*. In fact, Marty probably wrote his last letter to me as SWF secretary before he died. *Revolt* published extracts from his book and this created quite a controversy within the SWF, particularly over Marty's role in Spain during the Civil War. Arising out of discussions, closer contact was also made with the ILP. The ILP, however, rightly took objection to a reference in a resolution carried at the conference in Liverpool which referred to the ILP as 'basically reformist' and 'a corpse'. Wilfred Wigham, the then general secretary of the ILP, made the point: 'We can stand abuse, we have had our share of it. But we enter into any closer federation with other organisations as a live revolutionary socialist party, or not at all'. I am afraid that the old language of abuse and name-calling dies hard in the socialist movement, and I know that both Harry and I were unhappy with what had been said.

The fact is that the SWF was premature and to some extent too sectarian and dogmatic in its approach to issues. It slowly but surely began to break up. Some members went to the Labour Party. Others dropped out of politics altogether. Some, like J. Britz, became officials of the ETU (Electrical Trades Union), siding with Cannon and Chappell against the CPers. Harry McShane became involved with Raya Dunayevskaya, an ex-secretary of Trotsky based in the USA, who, as F. Forrest, had been connected politically with C.L.R. James. Raya Dunayevskaya wrote a book, *Freedom and Marxism*, which was based upon a development of Hegelian philosophy. This book had a considerable effect on Harry. Thereafter, he regularly wrote for *News and Letters*, the Marxist-Humanist journal in the USA.

After a period, and after great difficulty, I rejoined the Labour Party, I trust, taking my intellectual baggage with me. Harry and

I always remained close friends. He once said to me that the Tribune Group of which I was a member in the early days was the best Labour left-wing he could remember. He was a great comrade, a great friend, a brave socialist and revolutionary. It was a privilege to have worked with him.

Glasgow's Housing Crisis
(i). Glasgow's Housing Disgrace (1947)
Harry McShane

Glasgow, by common consent, is a great city, though there is room for disagreement regarding what its greatness consists of. There is much in Glasgow that favours the picture of greatness which our civic dignitaries like to paint.

It is when we take a glance at the housing conditions that we see a different kind of picture. We then see tragedies which would tax the efforts of a thousand Shakespeares to portray in an adequate manner. It is not possible to appreciate properly the amount of suffering caused by the housing shortage, but unless we know something of this we will not see how urgent the problem is.

Thousands of families are denied a decent home life because of the bad housing conditions. In some houses, three, four and five persons share the same bed because there is no room for beds. Children, in many cases, are familiar with the sight of rats because the houses in which they live are rat-infested. Young people living in old dilapidated properties cannot tell their friends where they live. There are overcrowded single-apartment houses with TB cases living in them,. There are young married couples unable to get a house of their own. The lack of proper sanitary facilities in many of the houses is another of the many evils connected with the housing problem. Overcrowding has spread everywhere, including the new housing schemes. This detracts from the picture of a great and prosperous Glasgow.

Councillors behave as if they were unaware of these conditions. Many of them are far removed from the problem and are apt to forget all about it as they shuffle, to and fro, between the committee rooms and the buffet in the City Chambers. They don't like to be reminded of it.

The late Miss Ellen Wilkinson, before the outbreak of war, was publicly rebuked because she made strong references to the housing conditions in Glasgow. It is necessary, however, even if the tender feelings of our councillors are hurt, to draw public attention to the question in order that something may be done to tackle it effectively.

It can be solved. Houses can and must be rapidly built. The type of house that lends itself to rapid construction is the house on which attention must be concentrated. Those who

THE MUNICIPAL MARTYR

THE SLUM LANDLORD (to his henchman, Disease): 'Ah, it's a hard and material age, with no sense of the sanctity of custom. Here we have these envious Labour fellows panting to destroy that dear partnership which has so long and so profitably united us!'

Pre-First World War Will Dyson cartoon caricaturing slum housing conditions (From the Daily Herald).

are building the houses must be given every encouragement to get on with the job. Houses must be given, first of all, to those in the greatest need of houses. They must be let at rents the people can pay.

These simple facts are easy to understand. Yet, strange to say, those in charge of housing seem to be unable to grasp them. It took months to convince Glasgow Corporation that temporary houses should be built. It took three years before they were compelled to convert empty shops into housing accommodation. It took several years before they agreed to employ private contractors as an additional means of getting houses erected. They have retreated but still resist proposals to speed up house-building. They cling to ideas formed many years ago when the urgency was not so clearly marked.

Experience has shown that those in charge of housing are incapable of moving forward on their own initiative. They require to be pushed. If the people push hard enough, and in the right direction, they will get the houses within a reasonable period of time. It is possible to outline a programme and to indicate the steps necessary to carry it through. Success then depends on how hard the housing authorities are pressed.

The present position

It will help if we spend a few minutes on the present position before dealing with the practical steps necessary to solve the problem.

It is now common knowledge that Glasgow requires a minimum of 100,000 new houses to meet the needs of the population. This figure was given officially by Glasgow Corporation in answer to a questionnaire sent out by the Clyde Valley Planning Advisory Committee in 1944. This did not prevent Mr James McInnes from stating, at the public inquiry on East Kilbride, that Glasgow's housing problem could be solved by the erection of 50,000 new houses. It is to the credit of Mr Joseph Westwood, Secretary of State for Scotland, that he demolished this statement by sound argument and showed that Glasgow required 100,000 houses.

The case for 100,000 new houses is established beyond doubt

and does not need to be laboured here. We would mention that the last report on the number of applications for new houses showed that there were 98,000 families on the waiting list. It is known that many families made no application because they hoped to be removed under slum clearance legislation.

The position becomes worse day by day because the old houses are more rapidly decaying. The shortage is becoming more acute and continually adding to the overcrowding. This all indicates that the estimate of 100,000 houses required by Glasgow is not an exaggeration.

Broken promises

There is no excuse for the failure of Glasgow Corporation to come anywhere near the housing output promised before the end of the war. The contrast between what was promised and what was actually achieved can be clearly seen from the following figures.

In the first post-war year we were to get 6,500 new houses. In the second post-war year we were to get 8,000. Had the promise been fulfilled we would have had by last May a total of 14,500 new houses, and we would now be working to get another 10,000 houses promised in the third post-war year. The actual number of houses built up to the end of last July was 3,684 of which 1,465 were temporary houses.

Had Glasgow Corporation not been compelled to accept temporary houses, by public opinion, we would have been worse off by 1,465 houses. It will be recalled that the Communist Party wanted 10,000 temporary houses built on some of the sites not likely to be used for a considerable time. The Corporation, when it did yield, agreed only to a total of 2,500.

It will be said that the failure is due to abnormal circumstances and this will be readily accepted by those who know nothing of Glasgow Corporation's declining output before the war broke out. A clearer picture will be seen if we place the Glasgow figures alongside those of Scotland as a whole, keeping in mind the fact that Glasgow's problem forms one-fifth of Scotland's problem.

The Government promised to build 50,000 new houses, in Scotland, in the first two post-war years. The total houses completed to the end of July, well over the two years' period, amounted to 30,382. Had Glasgow completed its full proportion of the houses, we would have had 6,076 new houses instead of the figure 3,684 already mentioned. It is clear that Glasgow did not keep step with the other parts of Scotland and that, no matter what angle it is viewed from, the failure to do the job is there for everyone to see.

Not having used our full proportion of materials, the bottom is knocked out of the argument that housing, in Glasgow, at any rate, was held up by a shortage of materials.

Present target

The target for 1947 has been set at 4,143 permanent houses. It is obvious that this target will not be reached. For the first six months, up to the end of June, the number of houses completed was 545, leaving 3,598 to be completed in the second six months of the year.

The output may be higher than last year. This will be due mainly to the fact that Mr G. Buchanan practically forced Glasgow Corporation, a few months ago, to accept a higher proportion of prefabricated permanent houses. It will also be partly because, for the first time, a serious effort was made to secure the help of private contractors who are working alongside the Direct Labour Department on the erection of traditional types of houses. This slight departure from the methods of the past has led to a slight improvement. A greater departure can lead to a greater improvement.

This will create new problems and will confuse those with a fixed mentality. It is possible, however, to get the results we are after without dispensing with the principle of Direct Labour as some of our councillors would like to do. The Direct Labour Department has started to play a minor role in housing, but this will be dealt with later. The important thing is that we clearly recognise the unsatisfactory position which confronts us at the present moment and take steps to get the houses in much greater numbers. Great possibilities present themselves, and no person has the right to accept responsibility for housing who is not prepared to make the greatest use of these possibilities.

Prefabrication

The idea of using mass production methods in house-building became popular during the war. It was in that period that we saw the greatest experiments in prefabrication. It enabled us to get temporary houses for a number of young married couples. About another thousand have yet to go up in Glasgow.

Prefabrication has been extended to permanent houses. Steel erectors are playing a part in the building of these non-traditional houses. Steel, concrete and other materials are being used to a greater extent than ever before.

Ayr County Council has designed a house which is pre-fabricated in all parts. An old shipyard, in Irvine, has machinery installed which cuts and shapes metal parts for this house. This very fine house is named the Lindsay house, after its designer. It is precision-built. The roof is erected before the walls, thus enabling work on the walls to proceed and inside fitments to be installed in wet weather.

There are about 20 types of prefabricated houses under construction in Scotland. Some, like the foam-slag house, have only prefabricated walls, while others are prefabricated in all their parts.

Glasgow Corporation made a slight departure when it asked powers to build a factory for the making of foam-slag walls. It was a very expensive factory and it will never give us the 2,000 houses per year which its sponsors promised. Foam-slag walls do not a dwelling make, but if the slabs were smaller the walls would be erected faster and the money spent on the factory would be justified.

Prefabrication makes speedy erection possible. Most pre-fabricated houses can be built within a month or six weeks. Traditional houses take on the average 15 months to build. It is clear that there must be a concentration on prefabrication if we are ever to overcome the housing shortage.

What to do

Nothing should be allowed to hinder house-building. The problem is particularly serious in Glasgow where housing has never been adequately dealt with. We must fight for increased output if the morale of the people is to be maintained. Even in the present crisis we cannot permit a cutting down in housing.

It will be gathered from what we have already said that we favour prefabrication and would ask for a concentration on this type of house. It is not proposed to stop building traditional houses. They also can be used. We must, however, put prefabrication in the forefront of our proposals to get houses.

Labour

Next to that we must take into account the fact that houses are built by human beings and that their everyday needs must be met if they are to do the job well. The working conditions of the building trade workers are a scandal. Private contractors only pay a guaranteed week of 32 hours. Welfare facilities, where they exist at all, are very far from satisfactory. This is not a pamphlet on working conditions, but it should be clear that unless the grievances of the workers are remedied, output will be affected. In addition to this, it is necessary that the workers be given an incentive to increase output. There is no need to apologise for advocating payment by results. There are signs that this is coming along, and the sooner the better for everyone concerned.

Many of those engaged on prefabricated houses are already working on a system of payment by results. This applies particularly to steel erectors who are members of the Constructional Engineering Union. Payment by results will secure greater output and should be adopted by everyone engaged on the building of houses.

There is also the proposal to set up Joint Production Committees. The point of view of the workers on the job is always valuable. The workers should be given greater responsibility on questions affecting output, and for that reason Joint Production Committees should be made effective functioning bodies, and where they do not exist they should be set up immediately.

Materials

There is a shortage of materials, and this is having a serious effect on housing output. There is a shortage of timber, and, to a lesser extent, a shortage of cement. It is questionable if anyone in authority has any right to talk about a shortage if the best use is not being made of the materials available. Everyone in Glasgow has seen cement and timber used on non-essential work. The matter has been raised with the authorities time and again.

Recently the Ministry of Works tried to explain the use of these materials for the Grand Hotel, a floor at Woolworth's Stores, and at an ice-cream factory. The Grand Hotel transaction was excused on the grounds that the Government wanted to encourage the tourist industry. The excuses advanced for the use of materials for Woolworth's stores and the ice-cream factory were even more trivial. Materials could be controlled and directed to housing and other essential work. The misuse of materials is criminal in view of the present position.

Trade negotiations should be opened up with Russia and other timber producing countries. By dropping our trade talks with Russia we lost timber for 30,000 houses. Cement production and the production of certain fitments in our foundries should be examined with a view of getting a greater supply of materials. Housing should be included among the priorities for steel, cement and timber. It will surprise many to learn that such is not the case at present.

Glasgow's Housing Crisis

Push the councillors

Perhaps more important than anything else is the need to press the councillors into action. They are too ready to accept cuts when they are proposed by the Government. The proposed cut in timber imports should be resisted by Glasgow Corporation, but here again the councillors will require to be pushed if we are to get results.

Let us sum up what is wanted if we are to get the houses:

1. We must look upon housing as being of urgent importance and a problem that cannot be shelved if the welfare of the people is to be our concern.

2. The urgency of the problem must be brought home to every councillor by means of deputations and demonstrations. To get this we must get the people organised around the housing question.

3. The fight for prefabrication must be waged in earnest. The various types of prefabricated houses available must be made use of.

4. Taking into account the fact that the building workers know more about house-building than the members of the Housing Committee they should be brought into functioning Joint Production Committees.

5. The people must identify themselves with the effort of the building workers to get decent conditions.

6. We should fight for trade with countries that can supply us with timber. We must fight for strict control over all materials available.

7. While uniting in a national struggle for houses, the special position of Glasgow must be raised. We must press the Government and the Corporation to get as many houses as possible this year and to set a target of 6,000 houses for 1948.

This programme will get the new houses, but there are other questions which require attention. Something must be said about the allocation of houses and the question of the unfit houses. But before going on to that let us deal, briefly, with the East Kilbride proposition.

East Kilbride

The members of Glasgow Corporation, without a single dissentient, made Glasgow a laughing stock over the proposal to build a new town at East Kilbride. East Kilbride will be the centre of a new town despite the opposition of the Glasgow councillors.

We cannot go into the matter in detail, but the proposal to develop a new town came from the Secretary of State for Scotland. He considered the housing and industrial congestion in Glasgow and North Lanarkshire, and concluded that East Kilbride should be developed as a means of easing that congestion. The defects of previous development in Glasgow, together with proposals made by the Clyde Valley Regional Planning Advisory Committee, were taken into account. He marshalled a host of facts in support of the proposition but they did not convince the members of Glasgow Corporation. The fact that some thousands of those waiting for houses in Glasgow might get a chance of houses in East Kilbride did not weigh with them.

Glasgow Corporation, along with a number of private individuals, objected. There was an inquiry and the objections got short shrift. The attempt of Mr McInnes, the Housing Convener, to convince the committee of inquiry that 50,000 new houses would solve Glasgow's problem was completely demolished. Facts regarding the housing needs of Glasgow were produced and most of these facts came originally from Glasgow Corporation itself. Valuable as these arguments are, it is not possible to reproduce them here.

The East Kilbride proposition will ease the problem in Glasgow by taking some of the people out. The opposition of Glasgow Corporation was an indication of how the councillors view the housing problem. We are desperate for the houses and we should place nothing in the way of easing the problem.

East Kilbride means more houses. It must be allowed to proceed.

Allocation of houses

In view of the widespread suspicion prevalent in Glasgow over the allocation of houses, there is a strong feeling that steps should be taken to ensure that the public know how the allocation is made. The suspicions have their roots in facts known to the people. Nobody believes that all the councillors who got houses were among those in the greatest need. There has been proved bribery of officials in the past. Things have happened within recent years which lead the people to believe that there is still considerable room for improvement.

The Communist Party raised this question with Glasgow Corporation some time ago. It was proposed that the method of allocation should be made public and that a list of those to whom houses are allocated should be posted up in the public libraries. These proposals were turned down, but, almost immediately, the Committee on House Management which was appointed by the Scottish Housing Advisory Committee recommended that the so-called 'points system' used in the allocation of houses should be made public. On this matter Glasgow Corporation has surrendered but they still refuse to publish the list of allocations.

The leaders of the groups in the Corporation receive copies of the lists and that is supposed to be a guarantee everything is perfect, but thousands of Glasgow citizens think otherwise and nothing is done to convince them to do the contrary.

It is not easy to believe that houses are allocated properly when it is known that there are cases of ten persons in a one-apartment house and that they have not yet been allocated a new house, while four apartment houses are let to families of two persons. There are thousands of families living in appalling conditions but they do not seem to be among the first when houses are allocated. The Councillors should learn that there are reports going about which reflect no credit on members of Glasgow Corporation.

This will continue until Glasgow Corporation reverses its present policy and ceases to act as a secret society concealing information from the citizens of Glasgow.

Rents

The rents charged for new houses prevent many working-class families from gaining any advantage from rehousing. Many families who have been removed to Pollok and elsewhere are finding it very difficult to make ends meet. Families living in bad housing conditions are scared in case they are offered houses at high rents. Others are not offered houses because the Housing Department officials know that they will be unable to pay the rents.

When the new Government subsidy was introduced, early in 1946, Government spokesmen said it was based on an average rental of 10/- per week. No permanent houses have been let in Glasgow at 10/- rental since before the outbreak of war. There have been some intermediate houses let, but the majority of the houses let have been ordinary houses. The subsidy from the Government should be increased to enable families to get houses at reasonable rents, but on this the Corporation has nothing to say.

Unfit houses

This problem is growing because houses are decaying more speedily than new houses are being built. There is legislation on the Statute Book to protect those living in unfit houses but it is not observed.

Glasgow Corporation does not take the necessary steps to inform the tenants regarding their rights. Mrs Jean Mann, MP, said recently that Glasgow Corporation had set up a committee to advise Glasgow citizens regarding their rights. Mrs Mann is wrong because there is no such committee in existence.

Tenants who apply for repair certificates are often met with hostility from the sanitary inspectors who investigate their cases. It is these inspectors who report to the Insanitary Areas Committee.

The Insanitary Areas Committee, which is composed of councillors, turns down the overwhelming majority of the applications. This has resulted in thousands of tenants living in unfit houses paying excess rents. The owners get 40 per cent over standard rent to enable them to carry out repairs, but in the cases referred to they carry out no repairs. Glasgow Corporation members are responsible for this because of their indifference to the question.

The Communist Party has given advice to hundreds of tenants, but the greatest obstacle to progress is Glasgow Corporation. Tenants who should be paying only 1914 rents are paying full rents because the Insanitary Areas Committee does not, in all cases, issue the necessary certificate.

The Corporation has power to prosecute property owners who do not provide proper sanitary facilities, but the property owners get away with it. This is a job for the housing associations. They should be on the job organising the people to secure repairs and press for amenities. The Corporation must be made to take action against owners who do not keep houses in a good condition.

Direct labour

Direct Labour is sound in principle. It has not been successful in Glasgow because of the limited outlook of those who have been in charge of the Direct Labour Department. To cover up its deficiencies the Housing Committee kept private contractors out. What is needed is that steps be taken to improve the efficiency of the department. It must develop prefabrication and secure the co-operation of the men on the building jobs. The Direct Labour Department must not be allowed to slip out of existence. On the contrary, it must continue and develop.

Vote for houses

The Communists have been the foremost fighters for houses in Glasgow. Many of the steps taken by Glasgow Corporation were forced on them by public opinion which was stimulated by the Communist Party. It is admitted that most of the councillors were reluctant to make changes and only yielded when forced to do so.

The Communists have been fighting from the outside. They want to fight inside. Nine vigorous candidates have been put up for the elections in November. They are fighting on many questions but housing is placed in the forefront. If elected, they will make Glasgow Corporation a platform for raising the urgent question of housing and from which they will endeavour to arouse public opinion. Their success will be your success. Vote for them and you will further the fight on housing and rents.

Housing cannot wait. It must be given priority. For that we must fight. Houses of all kinds must be built. The rents must be reasonable. Old houses must be kept in a state of repair. The list of those getting houses must be published.

Racketeering of every kind in housing must be brought to an end. These are some of the outstanding things for which we must fight:

Organise on housing! Fight on housing! Vote on housing!
As many houses as possible before December.
Six thousand houses in 1948.

CHAPTER 3

(ii). Gorbals is not Paradise (1946)

Harry McShane

It is a hundred years since Gorbals was annexed to Glasgow, but it looks as if 1946 will pass without a celebration of the event. That is as it should be, the progress made does not call for the lighting of a single bonfire.

The great scientific and technical advancement of the last hundred years is not reflected in the conditions of the people of Gorbals. There is nothing in the appearance of the district that would indicate progress. It might be possible to paint a beautiful picture of Gorbals, providing the painter kept as far away from the district as possible. The less he saw of the real Gorbals, the better the picture.

A stranger could easily be deceived on hearing the street names in a part of the district. We have Cavendish, Bedford, Cumberland, Oxford, Portland, Salisbury, Norfolk, Surrey and Warwick Streets. In addition, we have Carlton Place, named after a mansion once owned by the Prince of Wales. These aristocratic names are accounted for by the fact that the district was owned by a greedy old fellow, Laurie, who named the district Laurieston, after himself, and the streets after his favourite dukes and earls.

There is nothing aristocratic about this closely packed working-class district with almost 10,000 houses, the vast majority of which are of one or two apartments. The streets are dark and miserable, and poverty is evident at every turn. It is questionable if there is another district in the whole of Britain with so much squalor and misery as exists in Gorbals.

In Gorbals there are diseases which seldom afflict the

aristocracy. Tuberculosis is more prevalent than gout. The bad sanitary conditions, the absence of trees and grass, the lack of recreational facilities, all make it only too clear that the amenities afforded the Gorbals people fall short of those enjoyed by the aristocracy.

There is little of an elevating character in the appearance of the place. Rows of tenements stand on each side of the miserable looking streets. Here and there, the streets are partly covered in by railway bridges over which, from time to time, trains rumble noisily along. There is a growing number of gaps caused by demolition of tenement buildings, just in time to prevent them falling on the inhabitants.

Gorbals in the limelight

Now and then the light of publicity is thrown on Gorbals. Sometimes the more seamy side of life is brought to the forefront, and the general public, in other parts of the country, are given the impression that the people of Gorbals are on a lower moral level than people elsewhere. Some time ago, a book appeared in which Glasgow was painted in a very bad light on the basis of alleged happenings in Gorbals.

A well-known opera company has staged a ballet which conveys a wrong impression of Gorbals. The people of Gorbals would resent the suggestion that the sort of thing depicted in the ballet reflects life in the district.

Recently, a newspaper made a fuss over what they described as vandalism in a Gorbals cemetery. The children of Gorbals did not have a bit of grass to play on, and, being children, they seized the opportunity presented to them when the railings were removed from the cemetery in Rutherglen Road. The newspapers saw vandalism where ordinary people saw children greedy for a decent place to play.

The people buried in that old cemetery would not object to children playing over their graves. It is not generally known that the cemetery was purchased by the inhabitants of Gorbals in 1715, with money raised by a voluntary tax. They were, evidently, a thoughtful and sociable people, willing to co-operate for a good purpose.

Those who would charge the children with desecration should know that, in 1882, Glasgow Corporation, in order to widen Rutherglen Road, purchased lairs at a cost of £680, removed the remains, and reinterred them in Cathcart and Craigton Cemeteries, at a total cost of £385. This was necessary; but we should not strain at a gnat and swallow a camel. The damage done to the tombstones by the children is regrettable, but the failure to provide the children with proper playground places a share of the responsibility on other shoulders.

Gorbals gets the limelight for the wrong things. A little limelight on the failure of the Corporation to improve the conditions of the people would be more to the point, and would perhaps bring better results.

The people of Gorbals

The people of Gorbals differ very little from people elsewhere. The overwhelming majority of them have to work for their living; and, since Gorbals is not an industrial area, a large number of them have to travel some distance to their places of work. Gorbals is where they eat, sleep, live and die.

The skilled workers, as in most congested areas, are in a minority. In times of trade depression the district is badly hit by unemployment, though a considerable proportion manage to secure steady employment.

Some of the people are in receipt of Public Assistance, and, since the vast majority of able-bodied unemployed in need of relief have now to apply to the Assistance Board, it can be said that most of those on Public Assistance have applied because of ill-health.

There is also a considerable number of shopkeepers and persons engaged in business concerns of moderate size. Very few of them are much better off than the average skilled worker.

It is true to say that living conditions vary, and the houses in the district provide varying degrees of comfort. Facilities for entertainment and recreation being limited, many families content themselves with what little pleasure can be provided at their firesides. For any other entertainment, worthy of the name, the majority of the people find it necessary to leave the district.

Despite these depressing conditions, the people of Gorbals are as good as can be found anywhere. It would be futile to deny that a certain amount of demoralisation exists, particularly among those who have succumbed to the bad conditions, but it would be a slander on the Gorbals people to suggest that demoralisation is widespread throughout the district.

There is undoubtedly a considerable amount of apathy, and this is accounted for by the fact that promises made by various candidates have not been fulfilled. Conditions have become worse despite many promises that they would be improved.

The slaughter of infants

Scotland is notorious for the high death rate among children under one year of age. The worst city in Scotland for infant mortality is Glasgow, and one of the worst districts in Glasgow is Gorbals. Of the thirty-eight wards in the city, Gorbals is either at the top, or second from the top, when, each year, the figures relating to infant mortality are made known.

The latest available figures are for 1945, when the number of children who died in Gorbals before reaching their birthday was 119.

Taking the ten years, 1936 and 1945 inclusive, we get a total of 1,420 children born in Gorbals who died within one year after birth. Here are figures for each of the years:

1936	186
1937	162
1938	130
1939	125
1940	148
1941	177
1942	113
1943	136
1944	124
1945	119
Total	1420

It will be seen that the figure varies from year to year, but it is always a high figure.

It is an established fact that the high death rate is due either to bad housing or poverty, and that in some cases it is a combination of both. There can be other causes for deaths among children, but where the blame is traced to carelessness of parents it can in most cases be shown that the parents themselves are victims of the bad conditions. The greatest factor leading to the high death rate in Gorbals is housing. About that there is no doubt.

Those who survive

Even when the child has reached and passed its first critical birthday, it is not guaranteed a healthy and joyful childhood. It will, in many cases, require to live in an overcrowded room, and that room will probably be in some old tenement which should have been demolished many years ago. The house may even be rat-infested.

What chance have the children got in a place like Gorbals? The schools where they spend a great part of their lives are far from suitable. At least one of them is infested by rats. There is, of course, the Hutcheson's Boys' Grammar School, but that being

43

a fee-paying school, few, if any, Gorbals children go there.

The school should be a clean attractive place designed to take the mind of the child away from the miserable streets and houses of the district. The next step in education, so far as Gorbals is concerned, should be to build decent schools.

Where do the children play? There is a number of playgrounds for the younger children. They are hard coarse playgrounds surrounded by tenements. There is one at the junction of Pollokshaws Road and Cathcart Road. No matter where the child lives, it must cross tramlines to get to this playground. The point we emphasise here is that the children are not provided for. Our City Fathers are neglecting the city children. We will continue to have the problem of juvenile delinquency until such time as we take the proper steps to prevent it. New schools and playing facilities should be provided for the children.

Housing in Gorbals

Let us look at the housing conditions in Gorbals. The fact that most of the houses are over a hundred years old condemns them as unsuitable in the light of modern requirements.

It is when you appreciate just to what extent they are behind the times that you begin to see how urgent the question of housing really is. The outside lavatories serving, in some cases, seven families, the presence of rats and other vermin, the wet walls and many other evils, drive home the urgency.

The fact that a rat is found in a child's cot in a house in Crown Street; or the fact that a man and woman and five children are living in a single-apartment house in Erroll Street, with rats and snails in the house; or the further fact that there is a tenement in Lawmoor Street with eight feet of water in the basement, and water coming in through the attic, and rats passing the children on the stairs, should be sufficient to spur us into action on the matter.

Nothing has been done to improve Gorbals by the Corporation. Their crowning effort in regard to housing took place before any of us were born, when they stuck a little tenement in Muirhead

Street between a railway wall and an old brewery. There are no housing plans for Gorbals. The old houses are, apparently, to be allowed to stand as long as possible, and only if they become an immediate danger will tenants be removed. Houses knocked down remain gaps. There is a report to the effect that one of the gaps will likely be filled by the erection of a dance hall. This is on a site which many thought would be used for housing in the future.

In desperation, many victims of the housing shortage have taken over old shops and endeavoured to convert them into housing accommodation. The effort in the majority of cases is futile. In one case an old rag store was let as a house. There is another in which a money-grabber let out a bathroom for sleeping accommodation. This is a deplorable situation which must have the attention of the Corporation.

The indifference of some of the Corporation members is seen in the fact that exceptionally good houses at the top of Hope Street, owned by the Corporation, have been leased to a furniture firm for a period of twenty years for storage purposes. Other Corporation-owned houses in Gallowgate and Trongate have been similarly let.

Houses are decaying, but the Corporation is slow to act. It has become almost impossible to have an unfit house condemned. Persons living in unfit houses are now among the 'non-urgent' cases. Slum clearance has become a thing of the past. This means that, unless we can force a change in policy, the majority of the people of Gorbals will end their days in their present houses.

This is fine for the factor, but it is very bad for the tenants. Much more could have been done in the pre-war period. It is estimated that the Corporation Housing Committee could have built thirty thousand more houses between the wars. Just before the outbreak of the war, the output kept going down year by year.

Since the end of the war the Housing Committee has resisted every proposal to speed up house building. They had to be forced to extend their building activities, and even now there is a great reluctance to break with the past. House building is still too slow. The slow progress is covered up by resurrecting, from time to time, the same old housing programme. The nearer it gets to the November elections, the more we will hear of this programme.

In this connection, the role played by the Communist Party in pressing the Corporation is recognised by all who have watched developments in recent years. At one particular period the Communist Party was alone in the fight for the conversion of suitable shops into housing accommodation and for the erection of temporary houses. The Communist Party made public, for the first time, the facts in regard to subletting in Glasgow, and in Gorbals, in particular. The Communist plan to erect 100,000 houses in five years has never been discussed by the Corporation. Repeated efforts to get a hearing by the Corporation have been turned down.

The refusal by leading members of the Corporation to listen to anyone outside their own circle is responsible for their utter failure to meet the needs of the people.

Dirty money

Connected with the subject of housing is the question of subletting. This does not refer to a person letting a spare room or rooms, but to the racket which has been started in many parts of Glasgow, including Gorbals.

Some of the most disreputable persons imaginable are reaping fortunes out of the misery of those families who have no homes of their own and who are compelled to take whatever accommodation they can get. House factors are using persons as 'principal tenants' to take responsibility for letting the houses out room by room. Since they deal only with the principal tenant they can conceal the fact that they are getting more than the ordinary rents for the houses. This enables them to escape many liabilities which they would otherwise require to face.

Sometimes persons who specialise in this kind of business get control of property which they use to the full for their own personal aggrandisement. Often, it is combined with money-lending and other means of making easy money.

The 'principal tenants' control the electricity. In some cases they take out the fuses at a particular time and leave the sub-tenants in darkness.

There are abuses in connection with gas and other services, all of which are used to enrich an unscrupulous section of the community. The Rents Tribunal, when appealed to, can fix rents; but in no other way is protection given to these sub-tenants. This demoralising business is going on under our very noses, but nothing is done to stop it. Legislation is necessary, but in the meantime steps can be taken by the Corporation in regard to the services under their control. Requisitioning would also be an effective check on the racketeers.

Paying the piper

When Gorbals was annexed to Glasgow, a surplus of £600 was handed over to the Magistrates of Glasgow. This surplus had accumulated in the hands of the Gorbals Statute Labour Trust after having cleared a debt of £1,000 incurred by an earlier Trust. The Magistrates of Glasgow immediately doubled the assessment of Gorbals although the streets of the district were in an excellent state of repair.

'Senex', writing in the *Glasgow Herald* at the time, said: 'Of course the whole assessment thus laid upon the barony of Gorbals is appropriated to recausewaying the streets of Glasgow proper with fine dressed granite stones.'

This has little or nothing to do with the present situation, but it is a fact that today, a hundred years later, while amenities are provided in many parts of Glasgow, no improvement has taken place in Gorbals although the people of Gorbals, like the people elsewhere, pay their full share of rates.

A householder in Gorbals, who perhaps has paid rates for thirty or forty years, does not share in the amenities he paid for. There is not a tree nor a plot of grass in the district. There is no bowling green in Gorbals. Decent schools are conspicuous by their absence. There is no public hall. More serious than all that, the houses built at public expense have brought no comfort to the Gorbals people because the houses were not built in sufficient numbers.

Many shopkeepers in the district have had a raw deal because the factors have dodged paying their share of rates and have placed a heavier burden on the shoulders of the tenants. Tenants are paying owners' rates in addition to occupiers' rates. Because of the illegality of this, the Corporation does not recognise the change and has raised the assessment so that the tenants are paying, in addition, rates on rates.

When this new burden was imposed on tenants of business premises the Corporation refused to discuss the matter. Only when the Corporation was asked to pay owners' rates for property they had rented from private landlords was the matter discussed. The Corporation then gave in. The Communist Party tried to get something done about it but the property owners got away with it.

It is inevitable that rates will rise as amenities are increased, but where are the amenities in Gorbals?

Glasgow plan

Glasgow Corporation has a fifty-years' plan which, of course, most of us will never see completed even if the Corporation carried it through. The first report was submitted in March, 1945, but not one part of it has yet been approved. If carried out it will mean that other proposals, such as the erection of a bridge at Finnieston, will be thrown to one side. The Corporation works that way.

The second planning report deals with housing and in this connection proposes to erect 207,000 houses. This report would be welcomed enthusiastically if it visualised a more rapid building of the necessary homes. Mr Bruce, the City Engineer, who has drawn up the plan, does not think we can reach an output of more than 10,000 houses per year. He does not say when he expects even that figure to be reached.

More serious is the fact that the Housing Committee members do not think that the 10,000 will ever be reached and Mr Bruce does not know whether his plan will ever be approved by the Corporation. The members of the Housing Committee smile cynically when anyone talks of building houses speedily and whatever they may say they will only move if pushed.

Plans for Glasgow as a whole would affect Gorbals. The City Engineer's proposal to connect Cumberland Street with Scotland Street is one of them. The removal of the railway bridges would follow if the railway stations were moved away from the centre of the city. Proposals in regard to Glasgow transport would also make a difference to Gorbals.

The changes must start with Housing and every possible step must be taken to bring about improvements as quickly as possible.

A plan of the new Gorbals should be prepared without delay and a start made on demolition and rebuilding. Use should be made of existing gaps. In addition to houses, open spaces together with community centres and other facilities should be provided. The schools, where the children spend so much of their lives, should receive special attention.

Housing is in the forefront and in this regard our standard should be higher when deciding whether a house is fit or unfit. Every house of the single-apartment or room-and-kitchen type is unfit. Every house without a bathroom is unfit. Every house without a separate lavatory is unfit. Judged by that standard how many houses, in Gorbals, would be left standing? There are many houses unsuitable on insanitary grounds which should be demolished speedily and the families living in them should not be regarded as 'non-urgent' cases one day longer.

We are told the cost of land is prohibitive, but already a good deal of land in Gorbals is owned by the Corporation. The financial return from property to the Corporation is higher than for any other ward in Glasgow. In addition, a good deal of house property is changing hands, and although much of it is on Corporation land, speculators are allowed to purchase the property with a view to getting their pound of flesh later. The Corporation could prevent this by purchasing the property themselves when it is being auctioned. Of course, there will be cases in which this is not advisable.

Let the fight on housing start now. The Housing Committee is reluctant to act where bad houses are concerned and the tenants are denied the advantages of the Rent Restrictions Acts because of this. The sanitary authorities must either give the necessary certificates or close the houses. We must insist on this.

The fight to remove the slums must be connected up with the Communist Party demand that house-building be speeded up and 100,000 houses built in five years.

Communist aims

Much has been said about the aims of the Communists with a view to misleading the people. Even people in Gorbals, who have known some of the local members of the Communist Party for many years, have been confused on the question of what the Communists stand for. Some ridiculous allegations are made against them.

For example, it is said that the Communists would destroy religion. The Communists, on the contrary, are the strongest advocates of freedom for people of all religions. The right to worship should be allowed equally to all denominations.

The Communists are said to be paid agents of Moscow. Their interest in Soviet Russia is based on the fact that the people of that country are endeavouring to build a new society on a socialist basis.

The Communists are charged with wanting to take away personal belongings. This is not true. They advocate the common ownership of the means of production so that no man will be in a position to exploit another.

The Communists want to build a new system of society without unemployment, war and preventable disease. They are not content to deplore the evils of capitalism – they aim at ending capitalism.

The future of the human race depends on making the greatest use of all man's scientific and technical achievements but this is not possible under a system run in the interests of a few. Only socialism can bring that about.

Man can rise to a higher moral and cultural level. He can change his environment and in doing so change himself. The Communists whose interests are bound up with the interest of the people, stand for the greatest change in history, but the people as a whole must join in to bring that change about.

First steps in Gorbals

The Communists, while seeing the need for a fundamental change, never shut their eyes to the job immediately in front of them. The Gorbals branch of the Communist Party asks the people in the district to unite on the following issues in a campaign which should start immediately:

1. The issue of certificates by the sanitary authority for repairs to be done in houses which need repairs. Condemnation of unfit houses. A start to be made by building houses on ground available.
2. Improvement and extension of public wash-houses. Open a day nursery for children. Replace the worst schools by new up-to-date schools immediately. Improve and extend children's playgrounds.
3. Build a public hall. Lay out a proper open space where old people and others can sit in comfort. Erect a decent hut for old men to gather and pass their time. Provide a recreation centre for young people.

These steps should be part of a plan. No time should be lost in making a start. House-building should come before all else but it is possible to provide the other facilities and build houses at the same time. If these proposals are carried through, Gorbals will be paradise compared to what it is to-day.

We should aim at doing all this within five years. It can and will be done if we clear away the existing apathy and fight as right-thinking men and women should fight when their future welfare is at stake.

CHAPTER 4
Does Red Clydeside Really Matter Any More?

Terry Brotherstone

In the 1980s, what looked like a systematic attempt was made to downplay the significance of what had become known to Scottish, British and even international historians as 'Red Clydeside'. Recently it has become clear that this challenge has been successfully deflected. A new consensus seems to be emerging – at any rate amongst some leading historians of Scotland – which acknowledges the significance of the events associated with Red Clydeside, but seeks to dissociate them from what is now perceived as the 'myth' or 'legend' that they involved a revolutionary challenge to the British state, and that, as such, they were related to a Europe-wide (or even world-wide) threat to capitalism as a whole.[1] Such a consensus should ensure a prominent place for Red Clydeside in future general histories of Scotland. My underlying argument, however, is that important issues raised by an older way of looking at these events are now in danger of being overlooked at a time when they are increasingly important. Red Clydeside should

---

*This chapter was completed well before I was able to read John Foster's 'Red Clyde and Red Scotland', in I. Donnachie and C. Whatley (eds.), *The Manufacture of Scottish History* (Edinburgh, 1992), pp. 106–24. Foster approaches an analogous task to that posed here in another, to some extent complementary, way. Foster's standpoint is, however, quite different from mine.

Another recent book, Willie Thompson, *The Good Old Cause: British Communism 1920–1991* (London, 1992) makes a major contribution to launching the discussion of Stalinism in Britain, which is one purpose of this chapter to encourage. Thomson's main title, in my view, is strikingly wrong-headed; and his account has serious omissions, not all of which can be attributed to his admirable striving for brevity and readability. But, in its own way, it is a scholarly start. For a brief but indispensable comment on *The Good Old Cause*, see Peter Fryer, 'A History with a Blind Spot', *Workers Press*, 319 (18 July 1992), p. 6.

not only be shown to deserve its place in the Scottish history books, it also has a central part to play in political discussion at the end of the twentieth century.

I

What are we talking about?

Under an entry 'Red Clydeside' in a reference book edited by Ian Donnachie and George Hewitt for those seeking basic information on particular events, movements and personalities in Scottish history since the Reformation, we read:

> The name 'Red Clyde' arose from over eight years of intense labour conflict in the Glasgow area, coinciding with World War I and its aftermath. This series of episodes has assumed legendary proportions . . . and its resonance is particularly strong on the Left . . .[2]

They go on to list a number of inter-war labour leaders who, at this time, were 'participants in what the government regarded as subversive activity': James Maxton (1885–1946), David Kirkwood (1872–1955), Thomas Johnston (1882–1965), Emmanuel Shinwell (1884–1986), John Wheatley (1869–1930), and 'the early Communist activists William Gallacher (1881–1965) and Harry McShane', who lived from 1891 to 1988. 'Another leading activist,' they add, 'was the Scottish revolutionary socialist, John Maclean (1879–1923).'[3]

Donnachie and Hewitt then list the main episodes as they see them. There was a series of conflicts during 1915–16, they say, over working conditions in the engineering factories, rents, and the 'dilution' of labour. (Dilution of labour was the substitution of less skilled workers, including women, for skilled craftsmen in jobs concerned with munitions manufacture – a process made possible by available new technologies which had been resisted by skilled trade unionists jealous of the living standards and degree of social stability which they felt should attach to their skills and status.) Then, say Donnachie and Hewitt, came the forty hours' strike of January-February 1919, when a struggle to meet the threat of post-war unemployment by demanding a shorter working week led to an incident following which 'the streets of Glasgow rumbled to the sound of tanks'. 'Finally,' they write, in the Clydeside area 'the General Election of 1922 saw sweeping Labour victories'. They conclude:

> While revolution may have been remote from the industrial troubles of the Clyde, the events of the period – seen by some as the glad confident morning of Scottish socialism – live on in legend.[4]

In his essay on 'Scotland 1850–1950' published in a three-volume work summarising recent work on British social history, the influential historian of modern Scotland, Christopher Smout, writes of the Red Clyde years:

> What did it all amount to? It is easy to see that the government and the would-be local Bolsheviks were wrong to imagine Glasgow as a second St Petersburg [sic]. But it is equally wrong to see in Red Clydeside nothing of fundamental significance. The conduct of the First World War presented to the workers an extraordinary demonstration of ruling-class stupidity and selfishness. It was, however, commenced [in 1914] with an enthusiasm that the working class shared to the full . . .[5]

However, continues Smout, 'the great slaughter' began at the end of 1915 and, with 'the introduction of conscription next year, disillusion set in . . .'

> The blame was put where it belonged: on discredited politicians and ineffective generals; on a church which blessed the war and which met tragedy with hollow sentiment; on employers who used the national crisis to make excessive profits and to introduce new work practices which raised productivity but . . . were designed to destroy long-held craft privilege; on [unfair] local rationing committees. . . .

The war, in Smout's view, led to an 'appreciable heightening of class consciousness', particularly amongst skilled workers:

> It confirmed their growing sense of doubt about the ultimate benevolence of 'the system', and gave credence to the socialists' identification of the Liberals as humbugs and of capitalism as

fundamentally exploitive. But the revolution hoped for under the ILP version of socialism, while basic enough in that it envisaged limited programmes of nationalisation, state aid for council housing, and home rule for Scotland, also owed a great deal to the old Liberal radical faith that when the people ('the masses') came to impose their will upon Parliament, the system would, in a fairly unspecific but quite sweeping way, be altered for the better. Few expected that it would be necessary to change parliamentary democracy itself, or use force to attain their ends, or to abolish property.

It seemed that what was needed, concludes Smout, was 'for working men to capture Parliament and a brave new world would follow'.

Finally, Michael Lynch in the most recent scholarly, one-volume history of Scotland, writes:

The legend of 'Red Clydeside' was born of efforts made, both by a small band of socialist enthusiasts and by a panicky wartime coalition government, to link together different episodes – industrial

Glasgow Rent Strikers, October 1915. (Courtesy of Glasgow Museums: People's Palace).

disputes, rent strikes and demonstrations – into a revolutionary conspiracy . . . the rent strike succeeded where industrial disputes failed, for it combined patriotism . . . with the pent-up animus of the peace movement, and it built upon the issue of poor housing which had been the most telling factor in the ILP's rising popularity in the years immediately before 1914. Two additional elements gave the movement a unique cutting edge. One was the notable role taken in it by women . . . The other was the overlapping roles played by unconventional institutions such as local tenants' associations and the Women's Housing association, which did not conform to the inbred stereotypes of conventional political or industrial democracy. . . .[6]

Lynch goes on to refer to the '*annus mirabilis* of 1919, when the Red Flag was brandished in George Square' in Glasgow, and when, in Cabinet, the Scottish Secretary, Robert Munro, spoke of 'a Bolshevist rising'. These events, he recalls, led William Gallacher, 'by then an orthodox Communist', to write in his *Revolt on the Clyde*, first published in 1936: 'A rising should have taken place. The workers were ready and able to effect it: *the leadership had never thought of it*'[7] Lynch then reflects:

This retrospective prognosis has etched a deep impression . . . A lost revolution has since become the talisman of a Left trying to retrace its own footsteps. . . .

Against this 'deep impression', Lynch counterpoises the reality of the rent strike of 1915 'which had galvanised an instinctively *laissez-faire* government into intervention in the market-place.' This, he insists, 'was a greater landmark than the revolution that never was in 1919'. And he concludes with the observation that:

There is a curious lack of connection between the chief events in the history of 'Red Clydeside' and its leading apostle. John Maclean . . ., who was appointed by Lenin in 1918 as first Soviet consul for Scotland, was singled out by the authorities as the most dangerous of the Clydesiders . . . The man described by Hugh MacDiarmid as 'the greatest leader the working class of Scotland have yet had' remains an enigma, not only the symbol of a revolution that never was but also the awkward reminder of a

Does Red Clydeside Really Matter Any More?

lost *Scottish* Left . . . [and] the chief exhibit in a Pantheon of Red Clydeside built after his death.

These quotations from Donnachie and Hewitt, Smout and Lynch serve four purposes. First, some of the points in them will be taken up in the course of this chapter. Secondly, they give a convenient summary of what is being referred to when historians discuss 'Red Clydeside'. Thirdly, they indicate that disputes over the significance of these events have something to do with whether or not they were harbingers of a social revolution which failed to take place. Finally, they make clear that, notwithstanding the general discounting of the idea of revolution amongst these authorities, none of them is in much doubt about the considerable significance of Red Clydeside in modern Scottish history.

This last point acquires added interest in the light of the publication by the Saltire Society, in 1991, of a small book called *Why Scottish History Matters*. It sought to 'form the bedrock of a major debate to secure the proper teaching of Scottish History in the Scottish schools'.[8]

The historian charged with surveying the significant trends in the recent writing of twentieth-century Scottish history chose to ignore the controversies about Red Clydeside. Maybe this is not surprising since that same historian, Christopher Harvie, had thundered as long ago as 1981: 'Forget the Red Clyde . . .'.[9] Yet the omission is worth commenting on, since Harvie was no maverick in his desire to move Red Clydeside down, if not off, the agenda of Scottish history.

In the early 1980s, as the Reagan-Thatcher decade dawned and the tide of socialism was said to be turned, the political historian Iain Hutchison praised Harvie's twentieth-century volume in the Arnold *New History of Scotland*, not least because in it, so Hutchison claimed, 'the myth of Red Clydeside is . . . elegantly and surely conclusively demolished.[10]

Readers of Iain McLean's pioneering full-length study, which appeared in 1983, were not allowed to get past the dust-jacket before being assured that their sensibilities would be disturbed by nothing more incendiary than the *legend* of Red Clydeside.

Militant Workers

And Henry Cowper, reviewing McLean's book for Scottish labour historians, averred that it was,

> an important piece of historical research . . . difficult to refute . . .
> [It] should put paid to the myth of 'Red Clydeside' which, even by
> 1918, had become a sour journalistic cliché . . .[11]

When I researched these matters in the 1960s, I concluded that Red Clydeside, actually *became* a rather lively topic of journalistic discourse in the early 1920s, in the aftermath of the arrival of the Clydesider MPs in parliament in 1922.[12] But the more important point here is that it is clear, some years on from this scholarly assault, that these writers were premature in their morbid glee. Of various challenges to what, it has been said, was, in the 1980s, in danger of becoming the 'new orthodoxy on the myths of Red Clydeside', one of the most significant to date is that contained in Alan McKinlay's and Robert Morris' *The ILP on Clydeside*.

The central purpose of this book is to provide – in the form of a series of essays – an overview of the rise, heyday, and fall of the Independent Labour Party in the West of Scotland from the 1890s onwards. But the role of the ILP in Red Clydeside is central to the story.[13] *The ILP on Clydeside* also raises questions about the current political significance of the events it examines historically.[14] And, by studying carefully a socialist party that was, for a considerable period, genuinely popular, the book helps to combat the recent tendency to dismiss as irrelevant, or of secondary interest, the study of left-wing parties on the ground that those which were attracting the greatest attention never had much support. Although the Morris and McKinlay essayists concentrate very properly on the ILP itself, their studies imply questions about, in particular, the Communist Party of Great Britain. The demise of the CPGB in November 1991 at last opened the way for serious analysis of its historical role, and it is important that this takes place. As recent work on the hunger marchers of the 1930s shows, many of those who devoted their lives to it were the most committed and courageous of class fighters.[15] They deserve that the history of Stalinism is unpicked in detail, not buried in the vague allusions which sometimes pass muster in academic work.

II

What exactly was the 'new orthodoxy' of the 1980s about Red Clydeside? What did it state, how did it seek to prove its point, and what guidance can a discussion of it offer those who scan the written record of Scotland's past at least in part to find clues as to their most rational course of action in seeking a humane future for the country and the majority of its people? In seeking answers to these questions, it seems reasonable to turn first to the writings of those who have done most to mount a well-researched critique of the 'new orthodoxy' demythologisers.

Robert Morris, in his introduction to *The ILP on Clydeside*, explains his and his colleagues' approach to Red Clydeside and the interpretations of the early 1980s as follows:

> In [its] early years . . . [he writes] the ILP became an increasingly effective operator in a network of socialist and other working-class organizations. . . .[16]

The idea of the 'network' is a key, in this view of things, to the role of the Independent Labour Party on the Clyde from before the first world war through to the 1920s; from the period of its relative weakness to its post-1917 expansion which was to leave Scotland with a third of the organisation's entire membership. In particular the 'network' is 'important for assessing Glasgow's working-class political history during the key years between 1914 and 1922' – that is to say, during the period normally associated with Red Clydeside.

To this concept of 'network' Morris counterpoises the idea of Glasgow as a 'Petrograd of the West', a label which, he says, 'has obscured the debate over the nature of Glasgow's working-class political history for too long . . .'

Such labels associating Clydeside with the Russian revolution, suggests Morris,

> have tempted historians to use an overdefinition of 'revolution' which is then used to ask us to 'forget the Red Clyde'. Iain McLean has shown that much of the evidence of class consciousness concerned fragmentary, episodic action which arose from 'craft

conservatism'. But while it is true that the people of Glasgow did not storm the Winter Palace every weekend,[17] they did join the ILP in increasingly large numbers once both the franchise and registration had been sorted out . . . One of the social processes which drew together the various rent strike committees, the episodic interventions of the Clyde Workers Committee . . ., the trades councils and industrial action was the networking activities of the ILP activists . . .

The various organisations and activities which contributed to Red Clydeside, in other words, would have remained unco-ordinated, and no greater than the sum of their parts, had it not been for the networking link-persons of the ILP:

> John MacLean [sic] may have criticised the ILP-ers as opportunistic but in Glasgow during those years there were many opportunities.

Morris argues, in effect, that it was the ILP that was mainly responsible for the *real* Red Clyde, which should presumably be understood, primarily at least, as the expression of the reformist, protest politics of that organisation. The confusion, the myths and the legends, it follows, should be attributed to attempts to make a connection between the Clydeside events and the Russian revolution. The reference to John Maclean strikes an instructively discordant note in an otherwise careful argument. It is unheralded, and involves an unhelpful pun which does nothing to clarify the reader as to what Marxists mean by opportunism. Maclean would not have been referring to the everyday meaning of the word – taking your chances – but to the outlook which holds the immediate gains of a particular section of the working class higher than the historic interests of the class as a whole, as Marxists had understood these interests since the days of the *Communist Manifesto* (1848).

Maclean's appearance in Morris's summary argument, then, is abrupt and unhappy. But, if I am right about the general line, it is no accident, since, certainly in my view, Maclean's central importance lies precisely in his struggle in practice to establish the interconnectedness of Red Clydeside with the world-wide historical process of which the Russian revolution proved, at that period, to be the climax.[18]

Morris goes on to comment on the outcome of the Red Clydeside years, and, by implication, on their lessons. Two developments, he writes, had a 'devastating' impact:

> After 1918 the ILP became a party within a party [as a result of the new constitution of the Labour Party which permitted it to recruit individuals directly], and with the formation of the Communist Party in 1920 was faced with a rival invested with the political authority of the Russian Revolution . . .

This 'double-closure' (Morris's term) within the labour movement meant that the terms 'revolutionary' and 'reformist' became 'mutually exclusive', and went alongside the 'rapid dissolution of the activist networks which had long been the source of the ILP's vitality . . .' In Glasgow this did not lead to the decline of the ILP; on the contrary, it was able to become 'the effective Labour Party on the ground'. In this Glasgow differed from other areas because of the local structure of the labour movement. The industrial unions, as opposed to craft organisations, were relatively weak, and it was they which formed the main basis of the new constituency labour parties in most urban areas. In the West of Scotland the sectional unions, co-ordinated by trades councils, remained predominant, enabling the ILP to translate its networking role into the service of the Labour Party. Even when Patrick Dollan and his supporters, who were to be the architects of 'municipal Labour Glasgow' following the 1933 local elections, decided to stay in the Labour Party after James Maxton had led the ILP to disaffiliate in 1932, the tradition bequeathed by the political culture of the 'network' was so strong that Dollan

> was forced to form the Scottish Socialist Party to ease the transition into the Labour Party for the many ILPers who did not follow Maxton . . .

One of Morris's co-authors in the study of the ILP, Joseph Melling, elsewhere sums up the making of the 'myth' of Red Clydeside and the creation of the 'new orthodoxy' of the 1980s as follows:

The early Communists drew parallels between the struggles on the Clyde and the revolts which swept Petrograd, Berlin, Naples and Barcelona . . .

Then, 'as socialists faced isolation in the 1930s', William Gallacher and others penned 'heroic testaments . . . partisan biographies and autobiographies', which 'influenced later generations of industrial activists', notably the Communist Party members who, as shop stewards, led the Upper Clyde Shipbuilders struggle in the early 1970s. By then:

> A fresh generation of literature from the New Left which drew on the experience of shop floor conflicts and rank-and-file politics during the 1960s and early 1970s, was appearing to construct a radical interpretation of industrial politics in the years 1900–26. Writers such as [Walter] Kendall, [James] Hinton, [Richard] Hyman and [Raymond] Challinor provided an influential, critical view of the formative decades of 'Labourism' and the mistimed foundation of the Communist Party itself. . . .[19]

Thus were created, according to Melling's view, the 'myths' which Iain McLean's *The Legend of Red Clydeside*, published in 1983 on the basis of research largely done a decade earlier, was intended to combat. These 'myths' had their origins 'in both the older and the more recent left-wing versions of the Red Clyde'. Iain McLean's response, suggests Melling, should be seen in the context of

> the findings of [Ross] McKibbin, [Peter] Clarke and other liberal revisionists who have documented the strength of pre-1914 Liberalism and the limited impact of socialism in British politics during the early twentieth century. . . .[20]

More up-to-date Marxist commentaries, adds Melling, share with the 'liberal revisionists' the desire to move

> the focus of debate away from industrial warfare towards electoral contests, acknowledging the continuities between liberal radicalism and the early socialism of the Scottish pioneers. . . .[21]

Melling goes on to point out that the differences in their interpretation of Red Clydeside between James Hinton, the radical historian of the shop stewards, and the 'liberal revisionist' Iain McLean are not so great as they at first appear:

> Whereas Hinton has argued that a minority of class-conscious shop stewards were able to overcome the mass of craft conservatism in the engineering shops and confront the Government with a powerful Clyde Workers' Committee . . ., McLean simply asserts that the great bulk of the tradesmen remained highly insular and were indifferent to the political ambitions of the small group of activists. . . . [McLean's argument is that the lasting] legacy of the shop-floor conflict was sectionalism and craft elitism and it was only when the industrial militancy of the war years faded that Labour could lay the real foundations of a new politics for Glasgow. . . .

Melling also indicates that Iain McLean's thesis rests substantially on a particular view of the nature of the British state: that far from being an essentially repressive 'executive committee of the ruling class', it was flexible and 'essentially neutral'. This argument is of course central to the interpretation, not just of Red Clydeside, but of the whole history of modern Britain. It is a measure of the significance of Red Clydeside in this history – that is to say the vital need critically to *remember* the Red Clyde – that the connections between its particular history and key themes in the more general story are so close and specific. It is no wonder that the interpretation of Red Clydeside has played a notable role in the work of historians who have attempted broad interpretations of the nature and evolution of the state and society in Britain during the twentieth century as a whole. I am thinking particularly of Arthur Marwick, the most important of whose books, *The Deluge: British Society and the First World War* (1965), helped – along with A.J.P. Taylor's Oxford *English History 1914–1945* (1965) – to put the question of Red Clydeside on to the agenda of historical scholarship; Keith Middlemas, who, before embarking on his grand surveys of the twentieth-century state, found it useful to deal with *The Clydesiders* (1965); and José Harris, whose 1977 biography of William Beveridge, the central single figure in the history of the Welfare State, required a considerable passage on Beveridge's role in the events on the Clyde during the First World War.[22]

For Morris and Melling, if I understand them, Red Clydeside was mythologised by leftists overimpressed by the Bolshevik revolution and the class and protest movements of the 1960s. For them, there *was* a real Red Clyde; but it was the struggle of class-conscious, politically realistic working people, organising within the basic parameters of British society for greater justice, community consciousness and a humane collectivism – a struggle co-ordinated above all by the ILP. Red Clydeside, as the Morris-Melling school interprets it, contributed to the achievement of the Welfare State, although it might have preferred to base its institutions on a greater and more efficient system of local democratic control. Theirs seems to be a Red Clydeside which fits the picture of a 'cautious [British] revolution',[23] accomplished after major reverses, by the Labour government of 1945–50 – a 'revolution' in tune with Webb's slogan, 'the inevitability of gradualness', into which even the Thatcher decade was able to make only partial inroads.

The central specific achievement of this Red Clydeside was the change it wrought in the private market in housing, thanks to the success of the rent strikes in the summer and autumn of 1915 which led to the passage of the Rent Restrictions Act. Some of Melling's main contributions to the understanding of Red Clydeside have been related to the rent strikes,[24] and Morris asserts:

> The rent strike of 1915 was without doubt the most important and far-reaching achievement of the Glasgow working-class during this period. . . . an achievement in which the networking and support functions of the ILP were vital. . . .[25]

An answer to the first two questions I posed earlier has, I hope, emerged. In a nutshell, the 'new orthodoxy', at least as it is seen by those who have done most to upset it, stated that Red Clydeside was a legend handed down by activists to keep their spirits up in times of retreat, that there was no real 'threat of revolution', and that what was important – namely, the emergence of the Labour Party as the second major force in parliament – only took place when the wartime unrest had been seen off and recognised as a series of disconnected episodes with their several specific causes. All this was 'proved', as those who might be called the 'new synthesizers' would see it, largely by making an Aunt Sally from the idea of Glasgow as the revolutionary Petrograd of the West that didn't make it, and then knocking it down with research, much of which is valuable in itself but which fails to address itself to the right questions. From the critique of this method a version of Red Clydeside has emerged in which it was a real phenomenon, contributing substantially to the development of Labour politics and the Welfare State, but definitely to be dissociated from the aspirations of Bolshevik internationalism.

III

What then of my third question, concerning the relationship between these disputes about the past and how different views about them may be connected with ideas about the present and future?

Those whose interest in Red Clydeside is at least as much political as it is historical – and whose feeling of outrage at academics seeking to dismiss it as mere 'legend' comes as much from the sense that socialism is being undermined as from their conviction that historical scholarship is being improperly deployed – will nowadays be likely to turn first to Sean Damer. In Damer's chapter 'The Red Clyde' in his recent book *Glasgow: Going for a Song* they will find an ebullient account which attempts neither to reject nor simply to restate the 'old orthodoxy' but rather to relocate its positive essence within an analysis of the evolving culture of Glasgow, making use of the most recent research. In his contemptuous dismissal of Iain McLean's account, however, it seems to me that Damer confuses one central argument. Dissociating himself from what he calls 'the romantic left', he goes round in theoretical circles over the question of revolution. Damer writes:

> Neither during the war years nor in 1919 was Glasgow in something called a 'revolutionary situation'. The mass of the working people were not Bolsheviks, nor were the vast majority of their leaders.

But Glasgow in 1919 was the nearest thing to a revolutionary situation seen in twentieth century Britain. One major mistake by the government could have led to an insurrection: a few strategic moves by the Red Clydeside leaders could have led to a local seizure of power by the workers. But these mistakes and moves did not occur. With one or two exceptions, like John Maclean, the Red Clyde leaders were not revolutionaries. . . .[26]

There is much of value in Damer's chapter – but it does not lie in his contribution to a theoretical discussion of the problem of the relationship between Red Clydeside and the world revolutionary events of the period. To say that the mass of working people were not Bolsheviks, and nor were their leaders, could apply as well to Russia as to Scotland, certainly for the greater part of the pre-revolutionary period of 1917. And if, on the other hand, a 'mistake' by the government, and a correct strategy by the workers, were the only things needed for a seizure of power, then presumably there *was* a revolutionary situation lacking only a leadership to realise it – precisely the argument of William Gallacher in the 1930s. Yet Gallacher's *Revolt on the Clyde* is presumably one of the 'romantic' accounts from which Damer – who seems to want to nod in the direction of scholarly scepticism at the same time as offering reassurance to socialist activists – is trying to distance himself. And the implications of 'a local seizure of power' need much fuller exploration; particularly since John Maclean had no such concept at this point, and, as is well known, was not even in Glasgow during the events of January-February 1919.

The critique of Iain McLean, I think, is much better approached in the manner of Melling and others, by locating his views within the context of what historians have called 'liberal revisionism', than by debating with him on the vexed question of 'revolutionary situations'. The trouble with the latter is that it can never be known for certain that one existed until a revolution has taken place. For even the most theoretically prepared, practically involved, and politically bold party, the making of a revolution involves a gamble: it is no wonder that historians, who are better equipped to analyse what did happen, rather than to speculate about what might have happened, tend to flounder when dealing with such matters. Of course 'revolutionary situations' are worth discussing, in a past as well as in a future tense. But, in the context of the twentieth century certainly, as this chapter argues about Red Clydeside in particular, such a discussion must be grounded in an analysis of international and not merely national or local developments.

For Iain McLean the British Labour Party's rise to the position of principal opposition/governing-party-in-waiting is the key development requiring explanation; and the rise of Labour is seen in a symbiotic rather than a confrontational relationship to the decline of Liberalism. It is not necessary to suggest McLean was doing anything intellectually improper to point out that this view was not simply an 'objective' correction of previous 'myth'. It was also very much of a piece with the attempt in the 1980s to construct a Social Democratic Party which sought arbitrarily to discard what it disliked in the Labour tradition (the fact that the Labour Party was the product of the trade unions and therefore of the class struggle itself) while maintaining what it found acceptable (Labour's essentially bourgeois liberal ideology and association with the Liberal Beveridge's welfare statist conceptions).

The logic of the Morris/Melling view of things is different from the 'liberal revisionist' approach. The transition to the Labour Party is here seen as a real class change. But it was a change based firmly in local tradition, local action, local consciousness. Again, without belittling the integrity of the thinking or the scholarship which has gone into the making of *The ILP on Clydeside*, it may be suggested that its general viewpoint has its own contemporary echoes. One contradictory aspect of so-called 'Thatcherism' is that it gave rise to a questioning amongst some reformist theorists of the efficacy of previously accepted forms of state socialism. The centralised state, which seemed beneficial under Clement Attlee and Aneurin Bevan (at least when viewed through the misty spectacles of nostalgia), in the 1980s allowed Thatcher to do her worst – and to do it in the name of liberty of the individual. Successful resistance to all this, it appeared, was not organised through the trade unions and the Labour Party but through local initiatives, of which the 'networking' activities of the anti-poll tax groups were the most clearly effective. A re-interpretation of Red Clydeside which not only adds substantially to our knowledge but also draws attention to the 'networking' political activity of the ILP – and indeed sees it as crucial to the whole experience – may seem timely indeed.[27]

The ILP on Clydeside, in my view, takes two important steps forward: we now know, in a coherent way, much more about a key organisation; and we are able to see its successes and failures in the context of the developments in the British labour movement. But judged against the so-called 'legend', its political emphasis arguably takes the debate one critical step backwards – by confining understanding again within a purely British perspective. In this important respect the 'new synthesis' concedes too much to the 'new orthodoxy' of the 'liberal revisionists'.

IV

There are several key questions which the striving for a new, commonsense synthesis of recent research on Red Clydeside might be in danger of leaving untouched or under-emphasised.

First, the historiographical origins of the idea of Red Clydeside lie in the work of serious contemporary commentators concerned to analyse what was happening to European civilisation in the aftermath of the First World War. Historians have the advantage of hindsight and access to at least some of the records. But, on the other hand, they work within the constraints of academic standards which, in the traditions of Anglo-Saxon scholarship particularly, are most easily met by narrowing their debates within the limitations of national or local boundaries, and to questions which can be answered with the minimum possible reference to causative influences outwith their own immediate fields of research. Contemporary commentators by definition lacked distance from events in which they were involved; but they had the great advantage of feeling a compelling need to understand the whole context of such events and to discover their root causes, whether they could make a watertight methodological justification of their procedures or not.

Some American commentators at the end of World War I, for example, showed deep concern as to whether Europe would be swept by the Bolshevik tide or could advance towards an improved version of US democracy. Arthur Gleason for one, in his *What the Workers Want*, saw the rapid implementation of a reformist socialist programme by methods relying on the English spirit of compromise as the only antidote to violent revolution in Britain; and, for him, the Clyde was the 'storm center' of the challenge which had to be accommodated.[28]

A very different book was *The Industries of the Clyde Valley During the War*, by the Glasgow economists W.R. Scott and J. Cunnison, published by the Carnegie Endowment for International Peace in 1924.[29] Scott and Cunnison stated that:

> The labour developments specially distinctive of the Clyde during the war period were of more than local or temporary interest. . . .

Nor did they doubt that there was a serious revolutionary element in the story. Revolutionary syndicalism itself, they felt, 'had proved a flash in the pan', but its influence lived on through ideas of industrial unionism which at that stage seemed a real challenge to the conservative order built around sectional trade unions. While Scott and Cunnison saw the movement on the Clyde as industrial rather than political, and found it relatively unaffected by the 'internationalism of Continental Syndicalism', their reasons for such an analysis were rather different from those of later analysts restating the thesis that modern Britain is immune from revolution. Although the Clyde movement as a whole was not in itself political, they wrote:

> Its fundamental position was opposition to capitalism whose power 'bent the whole life of the community, political, educational, religious, and social, to its own ends'. Capitalism therefore must be abolished, and to that end the first step was the education of the worker in 'working-class economics'. Hence increasing numbers on the Clyde turned to Marx, because they found in him convincing proof of their belief in the evil of capitalism and the reality of class-war . . .

For Scott and Cunnison this was not political in the sense that the answer proposed, for the majority, was not the reform or transformation of the state but workers' control of their own industries; a solution which involved the overcoming of sectional jealousies fostered by craft unions and the building of a rank-and-file leadership. And what separated the Clyde workers from what seemed to these observers the characteristics of politics was the care with which, 'even in this revolutionary period',

proposals for the reorganisation of industry are elaborated. To the [Continental] Syndicalist, the general strike is the fulfilment; to the Clyde revolutionary, the general strike, so far as it was in the programme at all, was merely the beginning.

Events on the Clyde, for Scott and Cunnison, reached their 'turning-point' with the forty hours' strike of 25 January to 11 February, 1919. 'For a time it looked as though the "revolutionary" element were to carry the day', but the strong action of the Amalgamated Society of Engineers' executive and the changed position of the engineers in post-war society prevented this. By the time they wrote in the early 1920s, Scott and Cunnison may have believed there was less fertile soil for revolutionary ideas on the Clyde. But that does not seem to have been because they had changed their views on the capacity of the Clyde worker to devise detailed schemes for the revolutionary reorganisation of industry. It was rather because they believed the industries of the Clyde, organised on the existing capitalist basis, faced a future 'greater even than a great past'. Only briefly, from the late 1930s to the early 1950s, was this optimism to prove even relatively justified. In the shorter – and the longer – run, one must look to other explanations for the failure of revolutionary perspectives to achieve widespread support.

Another contemporary commentator was William Bolitho. His articles in *The Outlook* in 1924, soon published as a booklet called *Cancer of Empire*, actually use the phrase 'Red Clyde' (it is not nearly so widespread in the sources as the suggestion that it was a 'journalistic cliché' would imply). In the aftermath of the electoral breakthrough of the ILP in the West of Scotland

Does Red Clydeside Really Matter Any More?

in 1922 and 1923, Bolitho spent some time amongst the slums of Glasgow and wrote:

> The Red Clyde, the smouldering danger of revolution in Glasgow, owing to the swift development of political affairs in Britain, has ceased to be a local anxiety, and become an interest and an alarm to the whole civilised world. The complacent days of trust in things as they are have gone since the world war and the Russian upheaval, and no State, however geographically remote, however seemingly secure in possession of an unshakeable constitutional system, can any longer be certain of immunity from violent, bloody change in its body politic . . .[30]

In one sense Bolitho's contemporary observation tunes in well with the analysis of Morris and Melling, in that it was the housing situation which he saw as the root cause. But the point is that, in his mind, the slum conditions of, for example, the Broomielaw were such that, in the context of his sense of international affairs, it still seemed an undecided question as to whether they could be tackled by parliamentary reforms like Clydesider John Wheatley's 1924 Housing Act and previous measures; or whether 'Revolution, that foreign harpy' was 'really lodged within the Empire, and in Britain'. If so, it was 'in Glasgow we should look for her'.

Something of the atmosphere of the period is conveyed in these accounts which is missing in historical analyses which belittle the international context that so moved contemporaries. Such work, even the best of it, often seem to rely on sophisticatedly revamped forms of the theory of 'British exceptionalism' rather than on grappling theoretically with the real contradictions thrown to the surface of capitalist 'civilisation' by the First World War and the Russian revolution. At the end of the twentieth century when the capitalist order is once again under reorganisation, it is necessary to re-examine, not least through the eyes of serious contemporaries, all the ramifications of that seminal period. My argument here is not about precisely how close a Clydeside-led British revolution was at any particular moment in the years after 1917. It is that a deeper understanding of the significance of Red Clydeside depends upon discussing it within a revolutionary – and, of course, counter-revolutionary – international context.[31]

All this leads to a second key question, which relates to the significance of John Maclean. Those who wish to dismiss Maclean as an irrelevant and unoriginal Marxist outwith the mainstream of British labour history can no longer do so on grounds of lack of information. Notwithstanding the efforts of recent biographers, however, Michael Lynch in his *Scotland: a new history* is perceptive in implying that Maclean emerges from the academic literature as an unintegrated enigma.[32] Yet this is surely not because Maclean was insignificant, nor because his significance is all that difficult to grasp. It is because Maclean's Marxist internationalism was central to his relatively short political life, and his intransigent commitment to revolutionary principles inevitably makes him seem often isolated from the general run of opinion. The idea that somebody could be so profoundly committed in practice to the concept that the Clydeside working class, notwithstanding its volatile, existent levels of consciousness, was involved in a potentially revolutionary world movement, conflicts with the prevalent ideological terms of reference within which British history is usually written; and is difficult for many historians to come to terms with.

I have argued elsewhere that there remains much to discuss about Maclean, particularly his concept of revolutionary leadership and his understanding of Bolshevism.[33] The need for this discussion seems all the more urgent in the light of the new political situation of the 1990s. What is required is not merely analysis of the extent to which Maclean understood Bolshevism, but a much more concrete grasp of what the Bolshevik party really was, and of how far it was understood internationally at all – either at the time or subsequently.[34]

A third important point is that the dismissal of the formation of the Communist Party of Great Britain as 'mistimed' cannot be allowed to pass without serious argument. There is a major discussion to be reopened here concerning the early years of the Communist International, prior to the mid-1920s when Stalin became increasingly dominant. So far as the formation and early history of the CPGB is concerned, this discussion was launched many years ago in a series of articles by Michael Woodhouse and

Brian Pearce, reprinted in book form in 1975. But that book, *Essays on the History of Communism in Britain*, was not much noticed at the time and has received little attention since.[35] The new circumstances of the 1990s demand that it be examined with fresh eyes.

Far from simply dismissing the CPGB's formation as an error, the argument must be addressed that Gallacher and others were quite right to see it as the necessary political culmination of a process, at the centre of which lay the events of Red Clydeside. It must of course be remembered that the Bolshevik leaders had a considerable job in convincing Gallacher of this at the time; and it is not surprising that John Maclean and others were shielded against the full impact of the arguments of the International's leaders by the fact that it was the theoretically unprepared Gallacher who returned from the young Soviet republic in 1920, behaving, so Maclean thought, like 'the gramophone of Lenin'.[36] Looking back from the standpoint of the 1930s, Gallacher tended to reduce the debate about Red Clydeside to an oversimplified 'if only the leaders had thought of revolution' level, and he introduced the *canard* that John Maclean became paranoid to the point of insanity (although not everything in Gallacher's account is so unhelpful). But if the approach of Woodhouse and Pearce is afforded serious attention, we can at least explore the thesis that the party Gallacher and others set out to build in 1920, under the aegis of a genuinely revolutionary, if still immature, Third International, was very different from the Stalinist organisation which the CPGB had become by the 1930s.

V

There now seems little danger of Red Clydeside being 'forgotten' by historians, though the 'liberal revisionists' of British labour history are likely to continue discounting its more inflammatory aspects. Considering the concerted attempt to suggest the subject itself had become redundant, a quite remarkable degree of interest in it remains. But this is only the starting-point for a new, and more explicitly political discussion; one which examines concealed assumptions and theoretical perspectives, and which sees theory and politics not as tediously abstract or prejudiced impositions on historical discussion. Rather they are essential if valuable historical work is to be relevant outside the seminar rooms and specialist academic conferences.

The importance of the 'networking' or co-ordinating function of ILPers on the Clyde seems to be well-established, and valuably so. I recall Harry McShane himself making a similar point when I spoke to him in the 1960s, although he did not use the word, and, at the time, this did not seem to me the most important thing to follow up. Certainly the events of the 1980s threw up once again the need to examine much more closely the detailed forms through which working-class – and middle-class – people organise and co-ordinate their struggles; and may define 'community' as the basis for collective resistance.

The history of the 1980s in Britain was not only one of Thatcher and 'Thatcherism'. It was also a history of determined and often imaginative resistance to what many in the middle class as well as in the working class saw as an openly capitalist offensive. And that resistance cannot be understood, lessons cannot be learnt from it, by separating off those parts of it which seemed, in a limited way at least, to have worked, from those struggles which, in their immediate outcome, were seen as defeats. The battles in defence of local government from the early 1980s on, the miners' strike of 1984–5 and subsequent industrial conflicts, were as much a part of the movement which, along with splits in the Tory Establishment, ultimately humiliated Thatcher, as was the anti-poll tax movement. Defeats are bitter for those who are involved in them, but from the point of view of understanding the history of the period, and drawing lessons from it, they are just as much a necessary part of the picture as short-term victories.

Such, I think, is also the case with Red Clydeside. The resilience and refusal of Harry McShane to capitulate to the comforts of careerism are not things merely to admire. 'Red Clydeside', wrote one obituarist, 'never quite passed into history while Harry McShane . . . was alive . . . his dream of a new social order never dimmed.'[37] But it was no mere dream: it was a

Does Red Clydeside Really Matter Any More?

consciousness of necessity. And Red Clydeside cannot be allowed
to rest passively in the history books now that 'the last of the
Red Clydesiders' is dead. Furthermore it is the whole experience
that has to be re-examined in the light of the collapse of the old
certainties, particularly those associated with Stalinism. Now
that the relative – but limited and temporary – success of the
reformist mainstream of the ILP has been properly recorded,
it is necessary to look again at the revolutionary currents, and
at the real history of Communist Party to which they gave rise.
Discussion of the crisis of leadership in the working class may in
the past have been vitiated by sectarian dogma: but that is not
to say that it does not remain the central issue for historical and
political examination.

Surely too, as even the British ruling class now grapples with
'Europe', it is clear that a rejuvenated understanding of all
this requires the Scottish, and British, labour movements to
be discussed in an international context; and that this should
be done with due attention to those, like John Maclean,
who – however isolated they may sometimes have seemed –
endeavoured to bring an internationalist perspective to men
and women fighting for what they perceived as their own and
their fellow-workers' rights – whether in factories, on picket
lines, in their communities, in meeting halls or on the streets.
In such a spirit, I suggest, the burgeoning research on Red
Clydeside should be examined afresh. From this point of view
Red Clydeside certainly matters . . . more so than ever.

NOTES

1. See the quotations below from recent works on twentieth-century
Scottish history. A different emphasis may result if one approaches the
study of Red Clydeside from the standpoint of British labour history.
In this field the discrediting of the politics associated with the academic
Marxism of previously dominant labour historians such as E.J. Hobsbawm,
has reinforced a buoyant current of 'liberal revisionism'. This is painstakingly
documenting the continuities of English radicalism; denying the reality of
class struggle and the potentiality of proletarian revolution in Britain; and,
generally, seeking to dispose of Marxism. Key texts, which provide excellent
bibliographical guidance, are J. Zeitlin, 'From labour history to the history
of industrial relations', *Economic History Review*, 2nd series, XL (1987),

pp. 159–84; and A.J. Reid, *Social Classes and Social Relations in Britain 1850–1914* (Basingstoke, 1992). For the general tone, see E.F. Biagini and A.J. Reid, *Currents of Radicalism: Popular radicalism, organised labour and party politics in Britain, 1850–1914* (Cambridge, 1992), particularly the editors' introductory chapter (pp. 1–19). For Reid, Iain McLean's *The Legend of Red Clydeside* (Edinburgh, 1983), notwithstanding the work referred to in this essay, remains a work of key significance, a 'challenging revision of the myth of a revolutionary labour movement in this region': see Reid, *Social Classes . . .*, p. 70.

The literature on Red Clydeside itself is now extensive. The *Scottish Labour History Society Journal*, since its inception in 1969, has carried material relevant to Red Clydeside – the most popular single subject to fall within its sphere – in a majority of its issues. For ongoing interest, in addition to works cited elsewhere in these notes, the following are amongst the most notable recent contributions. Joseph Melling, 'Whatever happened to Red Clydeside? Industrial conflict and the politics of skill in the first world war', *International Review of Social History*, XXXV (1990), pp. 3–32, argues that, while emphasis on 'the limited progress of revolutionary politics and the presence of a powerful sectionalism in the industrial workforce' is 'now commonplace' nevertheless 'the struggle of skilled workers made an important contribution to the growth of Labour politics on the Clyde'. See also Melling's 'Clydeside rent struggles and the making of Labour politics in Scotland, 1900–39', in R. Rodgers (ed.) *Scottish Housing in the Twentieth Century* (Leicester, 1989), pp. 54–88.

John Foster, 'Strike action and working class politics on Clydeside 1914–1919', *International Review of Social History*, XXXV (1990), pp. 33–70, is an important intervention which, in its own way, puts back on the agenda of Red Clydeside issues both of revolutionary leadership and Marxist historical analysis. Foster analyses strike activity, particularly in the Clydeside shipyards, up to the 1919 general strike and against I. McLean and Reid, who either minimise wartime militancy or suggest it led to a strengthening of reformist social democracy, argues that 'a limited but significant radicalisation did occur', and that more workers on Clydeside than elsewhere in Britain drew 'socialist rather than social democratic' conclusions from their experiences. Foster concludes 'that the missing ingredient in Britain was not so much an effective political party. . . . It was more the politico-economic soil in which socialist forces could grow'. This seems to me a statement of, at best, limited value until the analysis is carried forward to study the immediate origins and early history of the Communist Party, and outwards to locate the particular problems of creating revolutionary leadership in Britain within the context of the early history of the Communist International.

Another example of continuing interest in the relevance of Red Clydeside is Mike Savage, 'Whatever happened to Red Clydeside?' in J. Anderson and A. Cochrane (eds.), *A state of crisis: the changing face of British politics* (London, 1989), pp. 231–43, which examines the contrast between the modern Strathclyde Labour Party and the Red Clyde tradition.

2. I. Donnachie and G. Hewitt, *A companion to Scottish history* (London, 1989), p. 161.

3. Short critical biographies of all these figures, except McShane, appear

Does Red Clydeside Really Matter Any More?

in W. Knox (ed.), *Scottish labour leaders 1918–39* (Edinburgh, 1984). The Manchester University Press 'Lives of the Left' series contains volumes on Maxton (by W. Knox, 1987), Johnston (by G. Walker, 1988), Wheatley (by I. Wood, 1990) and Maclean (by B. Ripley and J. McHugh, 1989). McShane's autobiography, written with J. Smith, is *No Mean Fighter* (London, 1978).

4. Donnachie and Hewitt, *A companion.* . . ., p. 161.

5. T.C. Smout, 'Scotland, 1850–1950', in F.M.L. Thompson (ed.), *The Cambridge social history of Britain 1750–1950* (Cambridge, 1990), I, p. 238. Further quotations from this essay are from pp. 238–9.

6. M. Lynch, *Scotland: a new history* (London, 1991), p. 424. Further quotations from this source are from pp. 424–7. On the relatively recent but dramatic impact of women's history in Scotland, see, e.g., A. McCleery, 'How do they manage in Scotland', *Books in Scotland*, 39 (1991), pp. 33–5.

7. W. Gallacher, *Revolt on the Clyde* (London, 1936), p. 234.

8. R. Mitchison (ed.), *Why Scottish History Matters* (Edinburgh, 1991), p. 92. C. Harvie's essay, 'Modern Scotland: remembering the people', is at pp. 77–87.

9. C. Harvie, 'Labour and Scottish government: the age of Tom Johnston', *The Bulletin of Scottish Politics*, 2 (Spring, 1981), p. 1. Harvie's oft-quoted injunction was not, of course, meant to be taken literally by historians. What, I think, readers were invited to consign to a liberating amnesia was not the facts of labour relations and political protest on the Clyde but rather the idea that these events had revolutionary implications requiring the recent history of Scotland to be analysed in the context of the international class struggle. Harvie's subsequent political evolution casts retrospective light on his wistful conclusion about Red Clydeside in his *No gods and precious few heroes: Scotland 1914–1980* (London, 1981), p. 23. He wrote that the 'revolution myth . . . obscures the real choice and the real loss . . .; co-operative decision making over innovation had been a genuine possibility . . .' This sounds rather as though we are being asked to believe that, if Harold Wilson had lived a generation or two earlier and worn a kilt, the 'white heat' of his technological revolution in which there was to be no room for restrictive practices on either side of industry might have triumphed north of the Tweed. Perhaps I have misunderstood the point; but Harvie was subsequently to embrace the Scottish National Party, having percipiently forecast its dramatic victory at the Govan by-election in November 1988. Since then he has made many interesting statements on Scottish and European politics, notably his 'Confessions of a bourgeois regionalist', heard by a conference of the UK Social History Society at Glasgow University on 5 January 1992.

10. I. Hutchison, reviewing Harvie, *No gods* . . ., *Scottish Historical Review*, LXII (1983), p. 103.

11. H. Cowper, reviewing McLean, *The Legend* . . ., in *Scottish Labour History Society Journal*, 19 (1984), p. 47.

12. T. Brotherstone, 'Red Clydeside', unpublished paper read to the Edinburgh University Historical Society, 14 October, 1969.

13. See, especially, J. Melling, 'Work, culture and politics on "Red Clydeside": the ILP during the First World War'; A. McKinlay, '"Doubtful wisdom and uncertain promise": strategy, ideology and organisation, 1918–1932'; and R. Morris, 'The ILP, 1893–1932: an introduction': chapters

4, 5, and 1, respectively of A. McKinlay and R. Morris (eds.), *The ILP on Clydeside, 1893–1932: from foundation to disintegration* (Manchester, 1991).

14. Morris remarks: 'It is fashionable now to downgrade the first Attlee government. . . . would that anyone could confidently say they had [its] strategies now . . .' He suggests that ILP history must be rescued from its submersion in a 'forward march of labour' historiography, tenable only until the mid-1970s, in part at least because, as David Howell's essay demonstrates, the Labour Party has continuously had to re-invent the ILP – as Bevanites, the Tribune group, Bennites and others, but none has ever seemed able to achieve that breadth of local base and intellectual-cum-parliamentary group that the ILP claimed before 1932.' Howell's essay 'The ILP and the Labour Left', concludes by exploring how far the history of the ILP may illuminate understanding of the relationship between the Labour Party and the Militant Tendency in the 1980s. See McKinlay and Morris, *The ILP* . . ., pp. 1–3; 228–9.

15. I. MacDougall, *Voices from the hunger marches: personal recollections by Scottish hunger marchers of the 1920s and 1930s*, 2 vols. (Edinburgh, 1990, 1991).

16. McKinlay and Morris, *The ILP* . . ., p. 5. The subsequent quotations are from pp. 5–7.

17. To which one might respond, 'Neither did the people of Petrograd!'

18. T. Brotherstone (ed.), *Accuser of capitalism: John Maclean's speech from the dock, May 8th, 1918* (London, 1986); and my 'John Maclean and the Russian revolution: a discussion article' in *Scottish Labour History Society Journal*, 23 (1986), pp. 15–29, reprinted with amendments in T. Brotherstone (ed.), *Covenant, charter, and party: traditions of revolt and protest in modern Scottish history* (Aberdeen, 1989), pp. 105–14.

19. J. Melling, review of McLean's *The Legend* . . . and other books in *Bulletin of the Society for the Study of Labour History*, 52(3) (November, 1987), pp. 54ff. For the 'radical interpretation' see especially: W. Kendall, *The revolutionary movement in Britain 1900–21* (London, 1969); J. Hinton, *The first shop stewards movement* (London, 1973); J. Hinton and R. Hyman, *Trade unions and revolution: the industrial politics of the early British Communist party* (London, 1975); R. Hyman, *The workers' union* (Oxford, 1971); and R. Challinor, *The origins of British bolshevism* (London, 1977).

20. See, for example, P.F. Clarke, *Liberals and social democrats* (Cambridge, 1978); R. McKibbin, *The evolution of the Labour party 1910–1924* (Oxford, 1974) and *The ideologies of class: social relations in Britain 1880–1950* (Oxford, 1990). See, too, footnote 1 above.

21. Melling, review of McLean, *The Legend* . . ., pp. 54–5.

22. A. Marwick, *The deluge: British society and the first world war* (2nd ed., Basingstoke, 1991) is a reprint which, however, contains a new essay by the author commenting on his book's significance: the section on Red Clydeside is at pp. 108–16; A.J.P. Taylor, *English History 1914–1945* (Oxford, 1965), pp. 39–40, 198ff; K. Middlemas, *The Clydesiders: a left-wing struggle for parliamentary power* (London, 1965), *Politics in industrial society: the experiences of the British system since 1911* (London, 1980), and his three volume study of Britain since 1940, *Power, competition and the state* (London, 1986, 1990, 1991); Jose Harris, *William Beveridge* (Oxford, 1977), pp. 215–27.

Does Red Clydeside Really Matter Any More?

23. cf. E. Watkins, *The cautious revolution* (London, 1951).

24. Melling, 'Clydeside rent struggles . . .' in Rodger, *Scottish housing* . . .; 'Clydeside housing and the evolution of rent controls, 1900–1939', in Melling (ed.), *Housing, social policy and the state* (London, 1980), pp. 136–67; *Rent strikes: people's struggles for housing in West Scotland 1890–1916* (Edinburgh, 1983).

25. McKinlay and Morris, *The ILP* . . ., pp. 11–12.

26. S. Damer, *Glasgow: Going for a song* (London, 1990), p. 107–39, especially p. 117.

27. Cf. particularly J. Smith, 'Taking the leadership of the Labour movement: the ILP in Glasgow 1906–1914,' in McKinlay and Morris, *The ILP on Clydeside* . . ., pp. 56–82; and her 'Labour tradition in Glasgow and Liverpool', *History Workshop*, 17 (1984), pp. 32–56.

28. A. Gleason, *What the Workers Want: a study of British labor* (New York, 1920), esp. p. 98.

29. W.R. Scott and J. Cunnison, *The industries of the Clyde valley during the war* (Oxford, 1924). The quotations are at pp. 138, 139, 150, 149, 150, 160, 192.

30. W. Bolitho, *Cancer of Empire* (London and New York, 1924), p. 13. The second quotation is at p. 22.

31. This argument is not without implicit support in some recent scholarly literature; e.g. L.H. Haimson and C. Tilly (eds.), *Strikes, wars and revolutions in an international perspective* (Cambridge, 1989) – especially parts I and V, the introductions and conclusion by Tilly and Haimson. See also D. Geary, *European labour politics from 1900 to the depression* (Basingstoke, 1991), which has a good reading list at pp. 73–4.

32. See the quotation from Lynch above (note 7). On Maclean, see B. Ripley and J. McHugh, *John Maclean* (Manchester, 1989); J.D. Young, *John Maclean: educator of the working class* (Glasgow, 1988) and a new biography published while this book was going to press, *John Maclean: Clydesdale Socialist* (Glasgow, 1992). While this wrestles with the question of Maclean's Scottishness, it also contains new international material and references relevant to the thesis on Red Clydeside being argued in this chapter. For my first reaction to Young's important book see a review to be published in *Workers Press* during September 1992. Still relevant, however, are N. Milton, *John Maclean* (London, 1973); John Broom, *John Maclean* (Loanhead, 1973); and N. Milton (ed. *John Maclean: in the rapids of revolution – essays, articles and letters 1902–23* (London, 1978).

33. Brotherstone, *Covenant, charter and party*, pp. 110–11.

34. This is why I disagree with Ian Wood who states that the reopening of debate about Maclean 'will certainly' centre on his 'relationship to what he came to recognise as the Scottish nation'. See I Wood, reviewing Ripley and McHugh, 'John Maclean' in *Scottish Labour History Society Journal*, 26 (1991), p.117. If it begins from there, well and good – and I note that Gerald Cairns's cogent and relevant appeal for Maclean's postwar Scottish political perspectives to be examined in relationship to his ideas on Ireland and India, rather than being dismissed as largely pragmatic, has so far been the most serious response to my own call for a new discussion on Maclean. See G. Cairns, 'John Maclean, socialism and the Scottish question', *Scottish*

Militant Workers

Labour History Review, 4 (1990), pp. 7–9; Brotherstone, 'John Maclean . . .', *Scottish Labour History Society Journal*, 23 (1986), pp. 24–6. But the discussion should *centre* on Maclean's internationalism, which is still far from widely understood.

35. M. Woodhouse and B. Pearce, *Essays on the History of Communism in Britain* (London, 1975), reprinted from *Fourth International*, IV–VI (1967–69); *Labour Review*, II–IV (1957–59); and 'Reasoner pamphlets', I (1957).

36. See, for example, John Riddell (ed.). *The Communist International in Lenin's time*, including so far (1992), *Lenin's struggle for a revolutionary International . . . 1907–1916* (New York, 1984); *The German Revolution and the debate on Soviet power* (New York, 1986); *Founding the Communist International . . . March 1919* (New York, 1987); and *Workers of the world and oppressed peoples, unite: proceedings and documents of the second congress, 1919* (2 volumes, New York, 1991); and R.A. Archer (tr.), *The Second Congress of the Communist International: Minutes of the Proceedings* (London, 1977), esp. II, pp. 44–5, 183ff. N. Milton (ed.), *John Maclean: In the Rapids of Revolution*, p. 225, quoting *The Vanguard*, December 1920.

37. T. Crainey, 'Harry McShane: the last of Red Clydeside's defiant dreamers', *The Scotsman*, 14 April 1988, p. 13.

CHAPTER 5

Roots of Red Clydeside: The Labour Unrest in West Scotland, 1910–14

Glasgow Labour History Workshop

The times we are living in are so stirring and full of change that it is not impossible to believe that we are in the rapids of revolution.
– *John MacLean to the Renfrewshire Cooperative Conference, 25 November 1911.*

1910 to 1914 were formative years for the young Harry McShane, then in his late teens and early twenties, an engineer and already politically active as a member of the Independent Labour Party. The year 1912, when Harry McShane celebrated his twenty-first birthday, was one of unprecedented industrial militancy in Britain as working days lost through industrial disputes reached a record of 38 million. This period was characterised not only by a series of major all-out battles between capital and labour in transport and mining, but also by a multiplicity of minor confrontations and skirmishes – insurgency, in other words, on a very broad front. This developed into a major challenge to the unilateral control which many employers had exercised over their labour force. It represented a mighty push by labour against what has been called 'the frontier of control' between management and workers.[1] At one level, this was a struggle by previously unorganised, lesser skilled, poorer paid workers – labourers, dockers, female textile workers, apprentices, carters – to obtain recognition of workers' trade unions and a collective bargaining dialogue as the mechanism through which working conditions could be improved and wages could keep pace with inflation. The artisans and stronger unions pressed further into the terrain of managerial prerogatives, challenging the right of engineering employers to operate their machinery as they saw fit, and in boilermaking and mining, the prerogative of capital to employ non-unionists. More alarming, perhaps, alternative socialist, industrial unionist and syndicalist ideologies were gaining support and were beginning to fracture the hegemony of capitalist ideas and – not least through newspapers like *Forward, Justice, Clarion* and the *Socialist* – expose the brutality and degradation of life and work under the *laissez-faire*, competitive market system.

This chapter investigates the patterns of industrial conflict in West Scotland over the years 1910 to 1914 and discusses several basic and commonly cited factors that are argued to have been the main causes of the labour unrest. It will be suggested that these factors individually did not precipitate the pre-war strike wave; rather, as argued by James Cronin, they came together to form an aggregate effect, a snowballing of accumulated grievances.[2] Firstly, however, we need to outline the dimensions of pre-war industrial conflict in West Scotland.

Strike activity in West Scotland

Between 1910 and 1914 British capitalism was convulsed by a series of major labour disputes and strikes. Strike activity and working days lost multiplied over 1910 to 1914 to four times the level recorded in the previous decade. Scottish workers participated fully in this strike wave, both through independent industrial action, as in the case of the Singer strike in 1911 and the Dundee juteworkers strike in 1912, and through active participation in nationwide conflicts of railwaymen, seamen, dockers and miners (see table 1).

In the heavy industrialised region of West Scotland, strike activity occurred across a broad spectrum of industries, with a notable concentration of unrest in mining, shipbuilding, engineering, metal working, transport and textiles. Major sectors of employment on Clydeside *not* participating in strike activity to any significant extent included retail distribution, domestic service, clothing, agriculture, fishing and the professions. A comprehensive trawl of two newspapers, the *Glasgow Herald*

The Labour Unrest in West Scotland, 1910–14

Table 1. *Principal Industrial Disputes in Scotland, 1910–1914*

Group/date	No. firms	workers	days lost
*Coalminers, Scotland, Feb – April 1912.	gen.	143,000	4,400,000
Juteworkers, Dundee, Feb – April 1912.	40	28,000	1,064,000
Dockers, Leith, June – Aug 1913.	25	4,000	172,000
Sewing Machine Workers, Clydebank Mar – Apr 1911.	1	9,400	141,000
Ironmoulders, Falkirk May – June 1912.	22	6,500	143,000
*Seamen and Dockers, Scotland June – Aug 1911.	gen.	13,000	113,000
Ironworkers, Falkirk May – July 1913.	gen.	3,085	104,890
Carters, Glasgow Jan – Feb 1913	80–100	3,500	101,500
Dockers and Seamen, Glasgow Jan – Feb 1912.	123	7,000	84,000
Miners, Motherwell Apr 1911 – Apr 1912.	1	265	83,210
Quarryworkers, Aberdeen Apr – May 1913.	73	1,542	72,474
Miners, Dreghorn July – Dec 1912.	1	450	58,050
Miners, Kilwinning Feb – May 1910.	1	645	55,470
Railwaymen, Scotland August 1911	gen.	16,000	54,000
Fishing Net Makers, Kilbirnie Apr – Sept 1913	6	390	50,700

Source: Board of Trade, *Annual Report on Strikes and Lock–Outs*; Supplemented with the Board of Trade, *Labour Gazette*; 1910–1914.

Notes: *These are approximate figures for numbers of Scottish workers involved in British disputes based on aggregate figures provided in H. Clegg, *A History of British Trade Unionism, Vol. 2, 1911–33* and census data providing the ratio of numbers employed in Scotland compared to GB in C.H. Lee, *British Regional Employment Statistics, 1841–1971*.

Militant Workers

Table 2. *Strike Activity in the West of Scotland, 1910–1914*

Year	1910	1911	1912	1913	1914	Total	%
Mining	3	16	8	15	11	53	20.3
Shipbuilding & Engineering	3	10	13	11	16	53	20.3
Transport	6	20	9	6	7	48	18.4
Textiles	1	6	12	2	7	28	10.7
Metals	1	2	12	3	8	26	10.0
Constructions	–	–	5	6	1	12	4.6
Printing	1	1	–	2	3	7	2.7
Chemicals	–	1	2	3	–	6	2.3
Timber & Furniture	–	2	2	2	–	6	2.3
Glass and Pottery	1	1	3	–	–	5	1.9
Municipal	–	1	1	2	1	5	1.9
Food	1	1	2	–	–	4	1.5
Retail	–	–	–	3	–	3	1.2
Miscellaneous	–	–	1	3	1	5	1.9
Number of Strikes recorded	17	61	70	58	55	261	

Source: The *Glasgow Herald* and *Forward* 1910 to 1914. Strikes enumerated within the geographical region comprising Renfrewshire, Dunbartonshire, Lanarkshire and Ayrshire. Industrial classification is that adopted by C.H. Lee's, *British Regional Employment Statistics*, 1841–1971.
Note: Figures for 1914 cover January to July only.

and *Forward*, from 1 January 1910 to the outbreak of World War One, produced the breakdown in industrial action shown in Table 2.

Given the high incidence of strikes over the first seven months of 1914 it could be argued that strike activity was sustained in West Scotland right through to the outbreak of war. The resurgence of strike activity through 1914 is somewhat at odds with the generally accepted UK model of industrial activity which, while registering continued unrest, indicates a tailing off of activity up to the outbreak of war in 1914. James Hinton argues that in 1913, nationally, there were 1,500 recorded strikes, more than ever before, and that working days lost were greater than any year since 1892.[3] Contrary to Pelling's indications of a 'successful stemming of the tide of successful strikes' – as a result of Lord Davenport's smashing of the 1912 dock dispute – the levels of unrest and militancy of workers was not generally weakened, at least within our geographical remit.[4]

The Labour Unrest in West Scotland, 1910–14

Our findings for 1912 and 1913 suggest that the nature of activity had changed to reflect both trade union successes and failures. The significance of the national docks' dispute, for instance, was not lost on workers. Rather than indicate acceptance of defeat, this event merely altered the conflict tactics. In 1913 a strike was more likely to be unofficial, and the workers unskilled than in 1912. In addition there is evidence that strikes were becoming shorter.

One of the major problems of standard analysis has been the poor picture obtained from reliance on the Board of Trade statistics for this period. Our preliminary findings suggest that the Board of Trade figures seriously under-represented the level of strike activity at this time. For instance, unlike our own survey, the Board of Trade figures do not include records of strikes which lasted less than one day or involved fewer than ten workers. Moreover, the shortfall in the Board of Trade figures can be partly explained by the failure of employers to release information to the Board. An official strike at Ardrossan harbour in 1912, which lasted ten weeks, did not become a Board of Trade statistic, as the Ardrossan Harbour Company, who controlled the port, decided not to complete or return the form sent to them by the board. The strike ended on 3rd January 1913, but in the Directors minutes for July of that same year the

Table 3. Comparison between Board of Trade Figures for Scotland, and Glasgow Labour History Workshop Figures for West Central Scotland, of Strike Incidence between 1910 and 1914

	Board of Trade	Glasgow Labour History Workshop
1910	11	17
1911	24	43
1912	41	70
1913	49	58
1914	6*	55

Note: Board of Trade figures are for the whole of Scotland, the GLHW figures are for the West Central belt only, comprising Ayrshire, Dumbartonshire, Lanarkshire and Renfrewshire. *1914 figures to August, from the *Board of Trade Gazette*.

meeting agreed that 'no information should be sent unless the company was compelled to do so by statute'.[5] This may well be but one example that could have been replicated in company boardrooms throughout the country.

To an even greater degree, therefore, our findings at this stage favour the analysis put forward by such commentators as James Hinton, that 1914 saw a dramatic increase in strike activity rather than a tailing off, as suggested by other analysts of the period.

The economics of unrest

There is little doubt that central to the question of what caused the labour unrest of 1910–14 were the problems associated with rising prices and stagnating real wages. A Board of Trade enquiry published in 1913 estimated that from the late 1890s until 1912 basic food prices had risen by up to 25 per cent, whilst wages failed to keep pace in real terms.[6] The *Industrialist* noted a similar trend and found that on average workers' wages had been 'reduced between two shillings and three shillings in the pound', or in real terms between 10 and 15 per cent.[7] Another Board of Trade investigation reported that the value of the sovereign had decreased by almost 20 per cent between 1895 and 1912, falling from a real value of 20 shillings to around 16 shillings and three pence over that period.[8] Fuel prices rose particularly rapidly. Coal prices in Glasgow had risen by 31 per cent between 1905 and 1912. The conclusion was 'probably the average increase in rent, fuel and food together may be about 10 per cent'.[9]

In September 1912 *Forward* reported on the findings of a Glasgow Trades Council investigation into the cost of living highlighting the rapid rise in wholesale prices of twelve main food items (at a time when food adulteration was still considered a serious problem). The prices are listed below for the years 1906 and 1912 and alongside the rise in prices is expressed in percentage terms.

The Labour Unrest in West Scotland, 1910–14

Table 4. Wholesale Food Prices, Glasgow 1906 to 1912.

Items	1906	1912	Percentage increase
Butter (per cwt)	94/-	115/-	22
Bacon	40/-	65/-	65
Sugar	16/-	21/-	31
Oatmeal	11/6d	15/6d	35
Marmalade	14/6d	19/6d	34
Jam	13/3d	18/3d	38
Split peas	5/6d	8/11d	62
Cheddar Cheese	54/-	76/-	41
Salt	2/1d	3/3d	56
Flour (per bag)	25/6d	33/-	29
Tea (per 100/lb)	95/-	116/8d	23
Raisins (per lb)	6d	9½d	46

Source: Forward, 21 September 1912

Such statistics emphasize the decreasing value of real spending power in Scotland. An STUC report of January 1913, to the Parliamentary Committee in the House of Commons, had little doubt that the root cause of the unrest was economic:

. . . For the past two years, labour has been clamorous and insurgent. For a decade wages have been almost stationary and the cost of living has rapidly increased . . . The nation now realises that the basic cause of the labour unrest is poverty . . . Poverty cannot be cured by conflict, but conflict indicates the seriousness of the complaint . . .[10]

Such contemporaneous reports indicate ample evidence, as Eric Hobsbawm argues, of the chief reason for the unrest being the perceptible stagnation or even decline in real wages.[11] In Scotland (and in Glasgow in particular) the problem was most definitely acute. The intimation is that many wage disputes in the period of the labour unrest were spontaneous reactions against escalating price increases and the erosion of the real value of wages. The explosion of worker militancy over 1910–14 was thus intimately linked to the bitter experience of many groups of workers during what Jim Treble has recently described as a 'crisis' period for Clydeside labour between 1903 and 1910.[12]

Militant Workers

Table 5. *Unemployment and Sequestrations for Non-Payment of Rent, 1900–14*

	I	II	III	IV
1900	2.5			10,818
1901	3.3			10,878
1902	4.0			11,409
1903	4.7	6.5	11.4	13,092
1904	6.0	9.3	16.0	14,517
1905	5.0	7.2	11.4	15,020
1906	3.6	4.0	7.5	14,528
1907	3.7	5.0	9.0	15,602
1908	7.8	19.8	24.2	20,858
1909	7.7	17.9	22.1	21,517
1910	4.7	6.3	14.7	19,556
1911	3.0	3.4	1.8	16,450
1912	3.2	4.2	2.1	11,239
1913	2.1	2.2	1.0	4,522
1914	3.3			3,660

Legend:
I   Percentage unemployed in Britain
II Percentage unemployed in Clyde engineering
III Percentage unemployed in the Clyde shipyards
IV Sequestration for rent arrears, Glasgow.

Sources: Column I. J.E. Cronin, *Industrial Conflict in Modern Britain* p. 229; Columns II–IV: J.H. Treble, 'Unemployment in Glasgow 1903–1910: Anatomy of a Crisis', *Scottish Labour History Society Journal*, No. 25, 1990, p. 39.

Those years were punctuated by two sharp economic recessions, as Table 5 shows, which hit the staple metal-working trades on the Clyde very severely.

Into this equation comes such considerations as bad housing, overcrowding and the concomitant factors of anxiety, disease and suffering, factors which combined to create considerable discontent. Indeed, in Glasgow, while rents did not generally rise, an acute housing shortage increased the problem of over-crowding, particularly after 1904 when there was a virtual cessation in housebuilding for working-class occupation. Between the census of 1901 and 1911 overcrowding rose in certain wards of Glasgow in contradiction to the general national trend. Joe Melling and David Englander both posit that such conditions led to a subterranean struggle over rents and the legal aspects of landlordism and made another significant contribution to a feeling of pressure on working-class living standards and lifestyle.[13]

In 1913 and 1914 the obvious downturn in sequestration levels would seem to intimate that the economic situation was improving. However, evictions in Glasgow between 1913 and 1914 actually increased. According to the *Glasgow Herald* evictions rose from 484 in 1913 to 738 in 1914.[14] This may have been due to the first dislocating effects of war. Nevertheless, it indicates how the lives of working-class people are intimately linked to and upset by sudden fluctuations in the economic cycle.

If stagnating real wages and living standards provided underlying grievances, changing product and labour market circumstances gave workers the opportunity to move on to the offensive against capital. In general, full order books and tight labour markets characterised the period 1911–14. This scenario, in turn, stimulated trade union membership, particularly within the unskilled sector, and significantly raised workers' collective bargaining power. Successful strike action further begot increased growth in trade unionism and raised workers' confidence in united action.

It may be advisable, however, not to base the whole analysis of unrest simply on the economic model. H.A. Clegg's own study into the period stresses such caution. He notes that earlier periods of similar unrest, in 1871–3 and 1889–90, did not follow periods of falling real wages.[15] Cronin also feels that the economic model is too narrow to explain outbreaks of labour unrest, especially 'periodic explosions of militancy', such as in 1910–14. In such terms the analysis of industrial conflict becomes simply 'a functional manifestation of breakdown in wage bargaining', and little else.[16] This theory thus takes little account of an independent will of labour, or, for that matter, of capital.

Capitalist Strategies: Work Intensification, Discipline and Control Mechanisms

There were other alienating tendencies at work during the 1900s and early 1910s which worked to fuel worker antagonism, bitterness and resistance on the Clyde. A significant worker grievance emerged in many sectors over attempts by management to speed-up and intensify work – to manipulate the customary wage for effort exchange. In crude terms this meant increased workloads; a quickening pace of production; the continual division of labour; breaking with the 'customs and practices' of the past, which arguably became welded into an accumulated sense of general discontent. From the late 1890s onward, states Cronin, 'almost all workers perceived some deterioration and intensification in their work . . . industrial concentration and management strategy were working to their disadvantage'.[17]

Work intensification was in part a result of increased competition between employers and from abroad. As a result, management sought to maintain their profit margins and sustain or expand their share of the market by attempting to change wage payment rates or introduce new work methods. Some of the more advanced employers experimented with the American inspired 'scientific method', or the 'Taylorist method'. A direct result of this type of strategy was the notion of the continual division of labour. This not only meant the continual de-skilling of the labour force, but through increased mechanisation, or significant changes in working practices such as payment by result, the process of production was speeded up, and this increased the feeling of worker alienation. Such developments prompted strike action at the Singer plant, Clydebank, in 1911.[18] However, scientific management methods spread very slowly. Before World War One British industry was still characterised by the small family firm for whom large-scale rationalisation of this nature necessitated large inputs of capital investment, which they were either unwilling or unable to risk at this juncture.

As a result, pressure at the point of production and work intensification was often identified in a less sophisticated manner. As often as not, 'stretch-out' took place within the parameters of existing technology and the traditional division of labour. At Weir's of Cathcart in 1914, a strike prompted this reaction from John MacLean:

The Singer Sewing Machine Company, Clydebank, around 1900. Scene of the all-out strike of March-April 1911 (Courtesy of Clydebank District Libraries).

> . . . This policy of rushing the men to get the work done more quickly not only supports our contention that articles tend to sell according to the time taken to make them, but shows that in the process the men are nagged until any excuse is seized to come out on strike. This clearly explains the strike . . .[19]

As an accompaniment to such methods, some employers increased their use of cheaper female labour – paid on average half the wage of their male counterparts. For example, the result of the 'ruthless rationalisation and shut down' programme adopted by the textile dyeing and printing companies in the Vale of Leven, was that 'only a minority of the male wage earners in the Vale were employed in the industry',[20] which, of course, drastically reduced the overall wage bill. In the textile industry – an industry differentiated by skill and gender – the better paid work was the prerogative of men. As in other industries, women – by virtue of their gender – were excluded from the most skilled and supervisory occupations. Indeed the hostile attitude of many trade unionists towards the employment of women tended to reinforce women's subordinate position in the labour market. Struggles over rates of pay were based on the concept of the 'family wage'. This meant that men were considered the breadwinners, needing to earn enough to keep a wife and family. Many single working women had to maintain a family, yet were not paid a family wage, while single men earned the same as their married male counterparts.[21]

Elsewhere, more intrusive supervision, cuts in the piece-work rates or longer hours, served further to antagonise workers. On the waterfront, while rationalisation was literally non-existent, there was a considerable effort to alter customary, time-honoured work methods. The reduction of squad sizes would be a classic example. The practice of cutting piece rates was widespread across many sectors of the economy. The Shipbuilding Employers' Federation, and the mineowners, continually attempted this.[22] Many women workers, already low paid, also had to contend with such methods. One example of this can be seen in the Caledonian Bakery strike in Glasgow in 1911 where attempts were made to cut wages by between three and five shillings per week.[23] As was noted above, such cuts were attempted at a time when those in work were already suffering under the pressure of increased prices.

Indeed, in some cases, even while employers were not attempting to cut wages, wages were not generally improved – often remaining at the same rates for many years. A strike of networkers at Kilbirnie in 1913 was due to a demand for an increase in the piece-rate which apparently had not risen in some 40 years.[24] Furthermore, it may be suggested that in those strikes where workers came out to force their 'supervisors and foremen' into the unions, for example, the strike of around 7,000 dockers on the Clyde in January–February, 1911, an attempt was being made to lessen employers' control at the point of production, by influencing supervision through the offices of the union. Indeed, this strike went further and demanded that clerks, measurers, watchmen and tallymen, as well as the foremen, all join the union.[25]

Workers were also fighting unrealistic bonus systems imposed to speed up production. Many had to contend with favouritism, where some workers were paid extra so as to cause divisions within the workforce and provide an incentive for people to work harder. Such concerns surfaced in a wide range of strikes in this period. A strike of coachmakers and bodybuilders at the Argyll Motor Works. Alexandria, was over an increase in workload without a reciprocal increase in wages.[26] At the Stewart and Lloyd Ironworks, Dalmarnock, 120 labourers went on strike because of the introduction of a bonus scheme which they maintained was impossible to meet, while at Bayne and Duckett's, Glasgow, in 1912, the introduction of machinery cut 'making time' by a third, simultaneously halving the piece-rates.[27]

Often the issue of work intensification is not easily identifiable as a cause of labour disquiet, but appears significant upon closer investigation. One good example would be the engineering and shipbuilding apprentices' strike of 1912. On the surface, this was a spontaneous revolt of poorly-paid apprentices against the new financial burden laid upon them by the passage of the National Insurance Act. This necessitated a weekly contribution of six-and-a-half pence by apprentices. However, Bill Knox has indicated how pressure on apprentices at the point of production was the underlying cause of the dispute: 'The action taken by the apprentices was less a conservative response to progressive welfare measures, but more a result of changing work patterns and increasing exploitation. Under conditions of rapid technological advance the productivity of the apprentice was rising, but his wages remained almost static.'[28]

However, like the economic factor, work intensification may be better classified as adding fuel to the fire, rather than acting directly, as a singular cause of the unrest. Whilst managerial driving and pressure at the point of production embittered many Clydeside workers in the pre-war years, the mechanisms utilised by capital in direct response to worker grievances, demands and actions served, in many instances, to further antagonise industrial relations and provoke renewed resistance and conflict. Capital was no monolithic, cohesive group and responses to labour initiatives varied considerably between employers and industries. Nevertheless, certain broad patterns in labour management-strategies over this period are discernible. Clydeside employers initially met the growing crop of disputes and strikes with force, coercion and intransigence. Importing non-unionist labour, blacklisting strikers, exploiting the full force of the law and threatening lockouts was the staple fare of the period. The propensity among Clydeside employers to introduce blackleg labour during strikes appears to have been particularly high, especially during the first phase. In the three years 1910 to 1912 we have positively identified blackleg importation in 29 out of 74 strikes, or two in every five disputes. This is more than double the rate of labour replacement in England during the labour unrest.[29] This may confirm a dogged and deep-rooted mistrust of unions and collective action amongst Clydeside employers.

In many cases managers and foremen used their own devices and contacts to recruit replacements during strikes, as in the Caledonian bakery in 1911, the Bonnybridge Co-op and during the refuse workers' strikes at Glasgow, Port Glasgow and Greenock in 1911. Similarly, the manager of the Hallside Steel Works in Newton obtained replacements for almost a hundred builders labourers in the summer of 1912, feeding and sleeping these men in the works to avoid problems with pickets. The correspondent in *Forward* gleefully noted that the Newton blacklegs were sleeping 'inside railway arches inside the works which for years have been used by the men as occasional free and easy lavatories'.[30] To a degree, the ability of employers to substitute workers during strikes was enhanced by the creation of labour exchanges, introduced from 1909. In addition, in providing police protection for blackleg labour during strikes, the state made a further contribution to employers' dispute-busting machinery.

Where employers were organised, the strike-breaking services of their employers' association could be drawn upon. The Paisley Contractors' Association provided such services during the carters' strike in March 1911, whilst at Ardrossan harbour, the Ardrossan Harbour Company actively sought the assistance of the Shipping Federation and the National Association of Free Labour to aid their efforts to attempt to create an 'open shop' in a Clyde port.[31] The services of an established network of Free Labour organisations and agencies were also exploited by other Clydeside employers. The North British Bottle Manufacturing Company, for example, responded to a strike at their works in Shettleston in May 1910 by obtaining youths through the Salvation Army and paying a well-known international 'free labour' agent, based in London (Peter Lamberti), to provide blacklegs from Germany, Russia and Holland. Needless to say none of these imported migrants were informed that there was a dispute in progress until their arrival at the works.[32]

Many other forms of labour discipline were exploited over these years. Police brutality, threatened evictions from employer-owned homes and the heavy-handed use of troops (as in the 1912 miners' strike) were allied with such devices as the lockout and legal action designed to intimidate the workforce. Legal actions against pickets appear with monotonous regularity during this period. Such tactics served only further to provoke workers by more clearly defining class inequalities and exposing the explicit integration of interests between state and capital.

Ideology and Solidarity

J.E. Cronin and Bob Holton argue that ideology played a significant role in the pre-war labour unrest, while others, like E.H. Hunt and Clegg place less emphasis on it.[33] Nevertheless, some analysis of the developing socialist, industrial unionist and syndicalist movements is a necessary prerequisite to the study of this period. This area of investigation is also important as it raises the problem of assessing 'consciousness' and labour's ability, or lack of it, to organise itself into strong industrial and political organisations. Although Hunt rejects the notion that ideology played a significant role in the period, pointing to the lack of support for syndicalism outside South Wales, others, including Dangerfield, believe that there was an upsurge in political activity, and unrest in the workplace 'was stemmed only by the firing of some bullets at Sarajevo'.[34] A manager at Weir's engineering works in Glasgow commented on how he perceived the problem of labour relations before 1914:

... The position just before the outbreak of war was that ... inroads in the power of management in the shops [workshops] had become so serious that, had the war not intervened, the autumn of 1914 would probably have seen an industrial disturbance of the first magnitude ...[35]

Clegg notes the 'significant' role played by syndicalists, or men who 'sympathised' with syndicalist ideas, in his own analysis of the period, but he is cautious not to over-emphasize the role of ideology. For all the solidarity shown by workers and the commitment by labour leaders, the role of ideology is not necessarily the 'cause of the unrest. Rather it was one of its manifestations'.[36] In contrast, other commentators accord greater importance to the role of ideology. Syndicalism, according to Richard Price, 'had made deep inroads into virtually every major union by 1914' and was by no means of 'negligible importance', as some suggest. It spread the notion of workers' control, making it 'widespread currency in the period 1912–22 and ... a serious alternative to nationalisation' as the main form of socialisation.[37]

Syndicalism was also a convinced critic of 'labourism', the Labour Party and of Parliamentary politics. Indeed, syndicalism was also critical of trade unionism, primarily when viewed as bureaucratic, unaccountable to its membership, and sectional in outlook. The fact that many of the strikes during the 'labour' unrest were very often unofficial, including examples of action which directly rejected union leaders' recommendations, is seen as evidence that the rank and file were questioning the role of the traditional labour leadership. A situation like this could arguably have proved fertile ground indeed for the fermentation of syndicalist or revolutionary socialist ideas, even as a proof of 'ideology in action'. The rejection of 'labourism' may have also helped matters. Could this have been the case in Scotland? The *Glasgow Herald* wrote as follows:

. . . It is evident that labour, to an extent that its accredited leaders would not have deemed possible, has got out of hand or has submitted itself to the guidance of men whose ability to release the forces of anarchy is no index of their power to undo the mischief they have done . . .[38]

In a later article this theme was continued when they criticised the orthodox leadership for bowing in docility to the 'leadership of the rank and file'. What seems to be implicit in these accounts is the recognition that labour was capable of exhibiting an independent will, possibly even a consciousness, through the rejection of orthodoxy.[39]

Another model used in analysing strike causation is the political-organisational one. Cronin offers this model as a credible foundation for the analysis of industrial unrest. The workers' ability to act collectively depends on their organisational strength: the stronger their organisation the greater their strength and the greater their ability to translate 'oppression into protest . . . grievance into strike'. Our evidence suggests that this could have been the case in West Central Scotland in the period 1910–14. It may be argued that no single element was the 'root cause' of the unrest, but rather various causes became welded together to form 'aggregates of discontent'. Cronin's analysis attempts to explain the labour unrest in this fashion, but does so in class terms: conflict arising from the contradictions between capital and labour. Given Cronin's 'favourable economic and political conjuncture' these 'aggregates of discontent' are translated into strike action, such as in 1910–14.[40]

Using Cronin's analysis, it may be argued that with a tight labour market and the growing organisational strength of labour, the economic conjuncture was favourable. In addition, with the wealth of alternative intellectual and ideological leadership and their repudiation of the traditional labour leadership and the growing reaction against the Liberal Government's social welfare legislation, it may be argued that the political climate was favourable. Thus accumulated grievances were united and expressed in strike action. High prices, lower real wages, work intensification or coercive employer strategies, persistent unemployment, the continual presence of underemployment, and class-conscious leadership came together to consolidate discontent. The resultant outburst may not have been the simple translation of discontent 'over specific evils and localised enemies, but on the performance of the entire system'.[41]

In his study of British syndicalism Bob Holton notes that many contemporaries perceived 'a syndicalist mood of revolt'. Having a sympathy with this syndicalist mood of the time, Ben Tillett noted a spirit of revolt which 'had seized even those of whom we had least hope'.[42] For Bob Holton, this translates into what he defines as 'proto syndicalistic behaviour . . . a form of action that lies between vague revolt and clear cut revolutionary action'.[43] This was apparent in many of the disputes that took place in West Scotland. Emanuel Shinwell, in 1911, reporting after the success of the seamens' strike of that year, noted that:

> . . . there was now recognition that sympathetic strike was an effective weapon . . . the seeds of revolution sown on Clydeside over the past few weeks are bound to have a far reaching result. Socialism has been rarely mentioned, but its principles and ideas have been expressed at every turn . . . one more link has been forged in the chain that binds labour together in an actual and living solidarity . . .[44]

There seems little doubt that much contemporary opinion viewed labour as indeed united and that ideology played its part in that unification process, even if today this is still a subject of heated debate among historians. Not only did intellectuals such as H.G. Wells and G.D.H. Cole perceive this, and labour leaders, such as Tillett and Shinwell, but also many members and officers of the establishment. George Askwith of the Board of Trade, David Shackleton of the Home Office, the Association of the Chambers of Commerce, the Employers' Parliamentary Council and many others expressed their fears and concerns over the rising tide of militancy shown by labour through sympathy, and direct action.[45] To such commentators the labour unrest was real.

Lines of communication were also tightening, aided by political propaganda and the process of organising labour. Not only did workers strike because they had seen the rewards such actions had gained other sections of the labour force, but also because they were more aware of levels of pay and working conditions experienced by other workers. In a strike of dockers at Ardrossan in 1912, the workforce exhibited an acute awareness of the wages structures of other dockers, not only at nearby ports, but in England and Wales also.[46] In the strike at the United Turkey Red works, Vale of Leven, in 1911 workers not only showed a remarkable awareness of contemporary wage rates in English textile areas, but also the terms and conditions of employment – especially the fact that female workers in Scotland were doing the direct equivalent of male workers in England, but were paid only one-third their wages.[47]

Our evidence suggests that wage disputes constituted 54.2 per cent of all strikes by women workers in the West of Scotland between 1910 to 1914. However, while wage and condition disputes were apparently the main cause of strike action at this time, trade union recognition almost always became a central issue too. Most female workers in Scotland at the beginning of the twentieth century were non-unionised. However, between 1910 and 1914 this situation changed considerably, particularly in the textile industry. This was mostly due to the work of the National Federation of Women Workers. It was the NFWW who agitated in the Vale of Leven, where, noted the *Lennox Herald*, the textile industry had 'been seething with discontent for some years'.[48] Disputes often escalated into much more than their humble origins suggest. One example of this type of escalation can be seen in the so-called 'mill girls' demonstration at Kilwinning in 1910, where, according to the *Glasgow Herald*, 'all the local people' were behind them, with local miners promising sympathetic support for 'their sisters'.[49]

This type of solidarity was to be seen to a greater degree in another strike at Kilbirnie in 1913. Female networkers there struck for over twenty weeks – the longest strike of any group of female workers in the West of Scotland during this period – engendering substantial sympathy action and virtually the complete support of the people of that town. The strike was eventually resolved in favour of the women, but its real significance may lie in the sympathy support the strike gained. The *Ardrossan and Saltcoats Herald* noted that there was considerable class solidarity shown by the miners, steelworkers and others who took part in the dispute.[50] Indeed, according to Eleanor Gordon, this strike 'contributed significantly to the mobilisation of labour in the area, on a class wide basis rather than a purely sectional one'.[51] Scottish women workers, Gordon argues, played an active and innovative role in what she terms 'the explosion of militancy' over 1910–14.[52]

When industrial action was initiated it often developed a momentum of its own, where the action itself aided solidarity and heightened political awareness. Such case studies, it may be suggested, can fit well into Cronin's model which attempts to explain the causes of unrest. Furthermore, there is little doubt that the ongoing industrial strike activity inextricably accompanied a great deal of political activity and propaganda. The strike leaders in Scotland, such as Joseph Houghton (of the Dockers' Union, who led the Ardrossan dispute, among many at this time), Emanuel Shinwell (of the Seamens Union) or Kate Mclean (of the National Federation of Women Workers, involved in the agitations at Kilwinning, Kilbirnie and the Vale of Leven), or the SLP leaders involved in the 1911 Singer strike, no doubt had a deep-rooted ideological strain to their trade union and organisational activities. Indeed it may be difficult to separate their political aims and identity from their industrial aims. This is not to say that the ideological commitment of Houghton, Shinwell or Kate Mclean was a syndicalist one, but there is little doubting their socialist commitment in particular and their political commitment in general. As can be seen in their many speeches during this period, all had an acute awareness of what constituted class divisions in their society.

This industrial, ideological and social solidarity owed something to the structure of trade unionism in Scotland – which had evolved along rather different lines from the rest of the UK. A stronger reliance on a federal system of organisation in Scotland had resulted in trade unions becoming collections of small autonomous societies and semi-autonomous branches with decisions being made generally at a local level. Even allowing for the amalgamation drive from the 1900s onward, there still existed between 30 to 40 distinct Scottish unions during the period 1910 to 1914. Moreover, as late as 1892, according to the Webbs, two-thirds of all Scottish trade unionists resided in the Glasgow area.[53] Industrial concentration favoured the West of Scotland and was reflected in the membership of the STUC. Indeed, because of this situation, there were demands to reorganise the Parliamentary Committee in 1905, as only two of the eleven members did not reside in Clydeside. By 1910, six out of the eleven members still resided in the west of Scotland. Even by 1914 over 58 per cent of all delegates to the STUC came from this area.[54] Moreover, a much larger proportion of Scottish trade unions were members of local trades councils than south of the border.[55] Therefore, Scottish trade unionism was highly federalised, more geographically concentrated and more directly activist led than was the case in England.

Conclusion

The achievements of the pre-war strike wave in the West of Scotland merit separate and detailed consideration. Lack of space precludes such an analysis here. Suffice to say, perhaps, that Clydeside labour encroached significantly into managerial terrain, pressing forward the inalienable rights of ordinary workers. One indication of the erosion of managerial prerogatives and the undermining of employer authority in the pre-war period was the growing failure to maintain the 'open shop' principle. The Lanarkshire and Ayrshire Miners' unions, with around 85 per cent of underground workers in membership, had for some time the only large group of workers able consistently and successfully to sustain strikes against the employment of non-unionists.[56] However, as the period wore on other workers managed to force their employers hands over such issues. Between 1913 and 1914, for instance, the boilermakers at both the Atlas and the Hydepark Locomotive

Works at Springburn, forced management to sack non-unionists on at least two occasions.[57]

More notable perhaps, were the stirrings of an offensive against the employment of non-unionists in the lesser-skilled occupations, leading up to the outbreak of World War One. In May 1914, there were three such strikes along the Clyde, involving carters at Rothesay, dyers in Paisley and crane and capstanmen at the Princes Dock at Glasgow.[58] The result of the carters' strike is unknown and the other two were unsuccessful, but this arguably shows the commitment of the workers to the principle of the 'closed shop' and to their unions.

In our concern to promote recognition of the important role of women, it was decided not to have a separate section – lest it should appear as an *addendum*, or that they were peripheral to working-class militancy. In reality, women did not hesitate to fight against exploitation and struggle for better wages and conditions in the workplace, like many of their male counterparts in the lesser-skilled trades, during the period under investigation. Their central demand was for trade union recognition. The dismissal of a member of the NFWW intensified a strike in the Kirktonfield Bleachworks, Neilston in 1910, and is but one of many examples which show women's determination to achieve trade union recognition.[59] Indeed, actions such as this may have contributed to the considerable increase in female trade union membership at this time – despite bitter employer hostility. Such examples go some way to dispel the myth that women workers were docile and reluctant to take industrial action.

Our evidence suggests that the ability of employers in West Central Scotland successfully to resist the challenge of labour during the period 1910–14 was seriously diluted. Those employers' associations who were still formidable and arguably more monolithic – such as in coal, engineering and shipbuilding – found the unions they faced able to match them in organisation and often exceed them in solidarity. The evidence implies that at this juncture employers in West Scotland may seriously have underestimated the power of the labour force, not only of organised labour, but the degree of support within many working-class communities too. Particularly menacing to employers was the fact that many of the working-class struggles of this period went beyond the boundaries of the workplace, as later seen in the rent strikes of 1915. Evidently the years of unilateral and autocratic capitalism in the West Central region of Scotland were numbered, and therein may be found the roots of Red Clydeside.

– *Ishbel Ballantyne, Louise S Christie, Ricky Devlin, Billy Kenefick, Arthur McIvor, Hugh Paterson, Irene Sweeney, Liz Tuach.*

NOTES

We would like particularly to thank Rob Duncan for his helpful comments on earlier drafts of this paper, Audrey Canning at the Willie Gallacher Library (STUC) for her generous guidance to relevant source material and the following, who all made contributions of one sort or another through the Glasgow Labour History Workshop to this project: Chik Collins; David Devlin; Fiona Emery; Les Forster; Eleanor Gordon; Bill Harvey; Clare Manning; Vasco Purser; Hugh Savage; Stephen Snee and Jim Treble. We would also like to express our appreciation to all those who responded to the first airing of this paper at the History Workshop conference in Glasgow, November 1990. This chapter is the product of an ongoing, unfinished collective research project which, so far, has involved an extensive trawl of the Forward and Glasgow Herald newspapers and individual documentation of every strike from 1 January 1910 to the outbreak of World War One. Lack of space and the immaturity of our research on this topic has precluded detailed analysis of a number of themes, including the role of women in the industrial militancy, the validity of James Cronin's 'conflict theory' and the unique structure of Scottish trade unionism. We hope, in the future, to rectify these omissions, broaden the range of sources and undertake a series of case studies of individual strikes during 1910–14. Anyone interested in becoming actively involved in this project are invited to contact the workshop, c/o the History Department, University of Strathclyde.

1. Carter Goodrich, *The Frontier of Control* (1920).
2. See J.E. Cronin, *Industrial Conflict in Modern Britain* (1979).
3. J. Hinton, *Labour and Socialism* (1983), pp. 88–9.
4. H. Pelling, *A History of British Trade Unionism* (3rd edn, 1984), p. 138.
5. William Kenefick, *The Labour Unrest of 1910 to 1914, with Particular Reference to the Ardrossan Dock Strike, 1912–13* (Honours Dissertation; History Department; University of Strathclyde, 1990), pp. 74, 81.

Militant Workers

6. Board of Trade, *Enquiry into the Cost of Living, Earnings and Hours* (1913).

7. *Industrialist*, October 1911, p. 4.

8. Board of Trade, *Investigation into the Changing Value of the Sovereign* (1913), cited in A. Tuckett, *The Scottish Carter* (1967), p. 117. See also R. Challinor, *The Origins of British Bolshevism* (1977), p. 63.

9. Board of Trade, *Investigation into the Changing Value of the Sovereign*, p. 235.

10. Cited in W. Kenefick, *op. cit.*, p. 2

11. E.J. Hobsbawm, *Industry and Empire* (1968), p. 159.

12. J.H. Treble, 'Unemployment in Glasgow 1903–1910: Anatomy of a Crisis', *Scottish Labour History Society Journal*, no. 25, 1990.

13. J. Melling, *Rent Strikes: Peoples Struggles for Housing in West Scotland, 1890–1916* (1983); David Englander, 'Landlord and Tenant in Urban Scotland', *Scottish Labour History Society Journal*, no. 15, 1981; R. Rodger, 'Crisis and Confrontation in Scottish Housing, 1880–1914', in R. Rodger (ed), *Scottish Housing in the Twentieth Century* (1989)

14. *Glasgow Herald*, 17 September 1915, cited in D.E. Englander, *Landlord and Tenant in Urban Britain, 1838–1918* (1983), p. 20. For more detail see Ian Muirhead, *The 1915 Glasgow Rent Strike* (BA Dissertation, History Dept, University of Strathclyde, 1991).

15. H.A. Clegg, *A History of British Trade Unionism Since 1889, Vol. II, 1911–1933* (1985), p. 24.

16. J. Cronin, *op. cit.*, p. 29

17. *Ibid.*, p. 59. For a general discussion of work intensification in the Scottish context from the 1880s see W. Knox, 'The Political and Workplace Culture of the Scottish Working Class', in W.H. Fraser and R.J. Morris (eds), *People and Society in Scotland, Vol. II, 1830–1914* (1990), pp. 143–5.

18. The Glasgow Labour History Workshop, *The Singer Strike, Clydebank, 1911* (1989). For a unique recollection of the continuation of such practices at Singer over the post-strike period, 1911–1914, see the Glasgow Labour History Workshop interview with David Burnett, in *Scottish Labour History Society Journal*, no. 25, 1990, pp. 76–87.

19. Nan Milton, *John MacLean* (1973), pp. 73–4.

20. S. Macintyre, *Little Moscows* (1980), p. 89.

21. See E. Gordon, 'The Scottish Trade Union Movement, Class and Gender, 1850–1914', *Scottish Labour History Society Journal*, no. 23, 1988, pp. 30–40 for a discussion of the family wage.

22. For example, at the Meadowside Yard in Govan and the Russell and Co. Yard, Port Glasgow. See *Forward*, 19 November 1910 to 17 December 1910; *Glasgow Herald*, 16 June 1911.

23. *Forward*, 30 December 1911.

24. *Glasgow Herald*, 23 September 1913; *Forward*, 16 August 1913.

25. *Glasgow Herald*, 4 January 1912; 5 January 1912; 17 January 1912; 22 February 1912.

26. *Glasgow Herald*, 29 November 1912; 3 December 1912.

27. *Forward*, 25 May 1912; 1 June 1912; 22 June 1912.

28. W. Knox, 'Down with Lloyd George: The Apprentices Strike of 1912', *Scottish Labour History Society Journal*, 19, 1984, pp. 22.

29. A.J. McIvor, 'Employers' Organisation and Strikebreaking in Britain, 1880–1914', *International Review of Social History*, XXIX, 1984, Part 1, pp. 11–14.

30. *Forward*, 3 August 1912.

31. W. Kenefick, *op.cit.*, pp. 39–45.

32. *Forward*, 21 May; 28 May 1910; *Glasgow Herald*, 25 May 1910.

33. Cronin, Holton, Clegg, *op. cit.* E.H. Hunt, *British Labour History, 1815–1914* (1981).

34. G. Dangerfield, *The Strange Death of Liberal England* (1961 edn), p. 351.

35. J. Melling, 'The Scottish Working Class and the Problems of Clydeside, 1870–1920' unpublished paper cited in T. Dickson (ed), *Scottish Capitalism*, p. 273.

36. Clegg, *op. cit.*, p. 74.

37. R. Price, *Labour in British Society* (1986), pp. 153–7.

38. *Glasgow Herald*, 16 August 1911.

39. *Ibid*, 28 August 1911.

40. Cronin, *op. cit.*, p. 58.

41. *Ibid.*, p. 99.

42. Ben Tillett, *The History of the London Transport Workers Strike, 1911* (1911), p. 6.

43. Holton, *op cit.*, p. 76.

44. *Forward*, 12 August 1911.

45. See G. Askwith, *Industrial Problems and Disputes* (1920); H.G. Wells, *The Labour Unrest, 1913*; G.D.H. Cole, *The World of Labour*, 1913.

46. Kenefick, *op. cit.*, p. 73.

47. *Glasgow Herald* 11 December 1912.

48. *Lennox Herald*, 9 December 1911.

49. *Glasgow Herald*, 24 November 1910.

50. *Ardrossan and Saltcoats Herald* 20 June 1913.

51. E. Gordon, *Women and the Labour Movement in Scotland, 1850–1914* (1991), p. 254. For a full account of the strike see Gordon, pp. 247–55 and S. Howitt, *The Kilbirnie Networkers' Strike, 1913* (BA dissertation; History; University of Strathclyde, 1988)

52. E. Gordon, *op. cit.*, p. 260.

53. S. and B. Webb, *History of Trade Unionism* (1950 edn), pp. 425–6.

54. These figures are derived from the Scottish Trades Union Congress Annual Reports.

55. A. Clinton, *The Trade Union Rank and File: Trades Councils in Britain, 1900–1940* (1977), pp. 189–198.

56. See, for example, the miners' strikes at Dreghorn and Bellshill; *Glasgow Herald* 5 July 1912; 18 September 1912; 1 October 1912; 30 November 1912.

57. *Glasgow Herald*, 26 and 27 November 1913; *Forward*, 13 June 1914.

58. For the carters strike, see *Glasgow Herald* 9 and 20 May 1914. For the dyers strike, see *Glasgow Herald*, 20, 21 and 27 May 1914, 9 June 1914. For the crane and capstanmen's strike see *Glasgow Herald* 22, 23 and 26 May 1914.

59. The woman dismissed was Jeanie McKinlay. See *Forward*, 13 and 20 August 1910; 10 and 24 September 1910; 1 October 1910.

CHAPTER 6

Independent Working-class Education and the Formation of the Labour College Movement in Glasgow and the West of Scotland, 1915–1922

Rob Duncan

On Sunday afternoons during 1915, in the crucible of wartime Glasgow – second city of the British Empire and key centre of munitions production – the schoolteacher and revolutionary John Maclean conducted the largest Marxist education class in Europe.[1] Since 1908, Maclean had held regular Sunday classes in Marxism in central Glasgow. Here, and elsewhere in the West of Scotland, Maclean and other comrades such as James MacDougall, had introduced many hundreds of workers, including shop stewards and other militants from large engineering factories, workshops, and pits, to the theory of the class struggle. Indoors and out-of-doors, the Socialist Labour Party had also been consistently active in the Glasgow area since 1903, running Marxist classes for its members and propagating revolutionary theory to the wider public.[2] From such classes, workers had acquired at least a rudimentary knowledge of the Marxist world outlook; its application to current problems at the workplace; and also some understanding of the capitalist system and its contradictions.

However, although Maclean's classes had always been well supported, it was only during wartime, when he courageously adopted an outright anti-war stance and enhanced his reputation as a revolutionary and outstanding public figure, that crowds gathered to hear his message. The Sunday class, which had moved to larger accommodation at the Central Halls, 25 Bath Street, attracted attendances of between four and five hundred, as Maclean turned his popular exposition of Marxist economics into a devastating critique of the imperialist war.

In 1915, those extraordinary classes continued to take the form of propagandist lectures on applied Marxism, with the usual scope for discussion at the end of the address; but their character had become transformed, becoming more like mass political rallies where working class solidarity and outrage were openly expressed against the capitalist war-mongers, the increasingly repressive government and state machine, and the officially orchestrated tide of anti-German chauvinism.

Although an important political phenomenon in its own right, the Central Halls' class in early wartime was only one of many manifestations of working-class discontent in the mounting political ferment in and around Glasgow and Clydeside. The extent and nature of this discontent remains the subject of keen debate among historians, but there is no denying the multiple unrest throughout the West of Scotland during 1915 alone, including a host of protest meetings against war speculation, price inflation and profiteering; the communal agitation of housing and rent campaigns; industrial militancy and the rise of a shop stewards' movement in key engineering plants in Glasgow; and the proliferation of advanced political and revolutionary ideas by small – but nevertheless influential – socialist groups, particularly the anti-war wing of the British Socialist Party (to which Maclean belonged) and the Socialist Labour Party (encompassing some leading industrial militants in the Clyde Workers Committee). A rising groundswell of discontent and protest within local communities in Glasgow and the West was being led and organised mainly by a network of Independent Labour Party branches, tenant groups, Co-operative Society branches, the Govan and Glasgow Trades Councils, and other trade union activists.[3]

By late 1915, Maclean and other socialists were concluding that the mounting tempo of the industrial and political struggles on Clydeside required extended efforts to reach, educate and equip thousands of principled, class conscious workers for the inevitable, fundamental confrontation with capitalism, and prepare the way for a co-operative commonwealth – the socialist society of the future. In this fresh initiative to provide political education for the needs of the class struggle, it is clear that Maclean and BSP comrades were in the forefront of a campaign to mobilise broad labour movement support for a Scottish Labour College.

The name and concept of a labour college was not the brainchild of John Maclean or of any of the comrades in Scotland. The idea for a college in Glasgow was to be based on the existing scheme of the Central Labour College in London. This venture had begun in 1908 in Oxford, initiated by a group of dissident worker students at Ruskin College. Dissatisfied with the curriculum, they formed the Plebs League to propagate a movement for a Marxist-oriented programme of workers' education, and to win labour movement support for a residential college which would be based upon this class struggle approach. The embryonic Central Labour College had moved to London in 1911, and by 1915 it was being funded completely by the militant South Wales Miners' Federation and the National Union of Railwayworkers. The College was also directly owned by the two sponsoring trade unions, while the outreach work for independent working class education was conducted by Plebs League activists in various parts of the country.[4]

The first notice of an outline proposal for the formation of 'A Labour College for Scotland' appeared in the Christmas 1915 issue of *Forward*. Also published as a leaflet, the circular indicated that the proposal stemmed from a committee which had been formed by members of the Central Halls' Sunday class.[5] After conducting an energetic campaign into early 1916, Maclean and the committee were rewarded by a large attendance and enthusiastic response at the preparatory conference called for Saturday, 12 February, in Glasgow. No fewer than 496 delegates participated, drawn from 412 working-class organisations and branches throughout Scotland, including co-operative societies, trade unions, trades councils and political organisations – namely the ILP, BSP, and the Women's Labour League (the women's section of the ILP). Significantly, Socialist Labour Party branches were not represented, preferring at this juncture to remain aloof from joint political education initiatives. However, John McLure, one of its leading Glasgow members, was present as an interested participant, as an individual member of the Plebs League.

Conference carried unanimously the motion for establishing a Labour college, and appointed a 32-member provisional committee 'with full powers to act until the first annual conference of the Scottish Labour College'.[6]

Earlier, the conference had listened to, and approved an address which had been prepared by Maclean and MacDougall. This manifesto outlining the principles and programme for a Scottish labour college was read to conference by MacDougall, in the enforced absence of Maclean who had been arrested on 6 February. Together, the circular of December 1915 and the February 1916 address to conference contain the original prospectus and manifesto for the intended Scottish Labour College. The address, which was later published as a pamphlet, *A Plea for the Labour College for Scotland*, is an impressive document, putting an eloquent, forceful and convincing case for the principle and implementation of independent working-class education. Here, it may be useful to provide a summary and interpretation of the plan, as stated in the founding documents, before attempting to examine the course of development in the early years of the scheme; the problems which blocked progress; and the extent of the eventual achievements against the original intentions for the project.[7]

Taking their lead from the Plebs League, the advocates of a Scottish Labour College adhered categorically to the concept of 'independent working class education'. The December 1915 circular was explicit in this regard, stating:

> The universities and other institutions for higher education have for their object the training of men and women to run capitalist society in the interests of the wealthy. We think the time has come for an independent college, financed and controlled by the working class, in which workers might be trained for the battle against the masters.

A key word and concept was 'independent'. It was understood as an uncompromising term of reference, meaning separate from, autonomous of, opposed to, and free from state financial control

– from the reactionary ideology and values upheld by the capitalist universities – from the employing class and their interests – and, indeed, free from any form of public funding or private sponsorship which would in any way endanger or destroy the independent, labour movement ownership of worker education.

This notion of 'independence' was thus construed as a fundamental class and political position. The working-class movement had to forge and control its own education, if only to defend itself against the wiles and depredations of capitalism. Workers had built trade unions as independent, basic, defensive organisations; and they had been forced to build their own independent political parties and organisations to combat the two capitalist political parties. They were now realising the need to build and sustain their own independent working class education, to counter the thought-control of the class enemy, its domination of the press and other media.

The struggle for workers' education was seen as a direct reflection of the class struggle itself, in which there were essentially two opposing camps – Capital and Labour. Education was an ideological battleground contested by those separate class interests. As such, the content and purposes of education and learning could not be neutral, impartial, objective, or value-free. For independent working-class education, the choice of educational provision and the application of progressive methods of enquiry were both crucial, and had to reflect, articulate and promote the aspirations and emancipation of Labour. To its proponents, the core and foundation of the curriculum were the study of economics and the history of the class struggle, both 'taught fundamentally from the labour standpoint'. As the only real alternative to texts and writings which denied the existence of the class struggle and which defended or apologised for capitalism and its values, 'our students must make the writings of Marx and marxian scholars the basis of their studies: otherwise the College becomes an expensive tragedy'.[8]

The perspectives and insights to be derived from Marxist theory would be used, whenever and wherever possible, to interpret the world, and serve as the foundation for criticising other ideas and theories. Thus the study of economics would be firmly grounded on Marxist writings, but would also involve a critique of orthodox and radical political economy. Economics was regarded as the key subject underpinning all the social sciences and, treated either from an overtly Marxist perspective or from a 'labour/working class' perspective, the primary objectives of studying this subject were to gain an understanding of the inner workings of the capitalist system, the reasons for working-class exploitation, the nature of the crisis of British and international capitalism, and also of imperialism. The study of economics from this standpoint was also intimately linked to gaining an understanding of the theory and history of the class struggle and of the general laws of historical development, emphasising the conflict between capital and labour in modern times, and the role of the working class as the gravedigger of capitalism.

A thorough grounding in the problems, history, theory and practice of trade unionism, labour law, and the co-operative movement were also regarded as essential components of the proposed College syllabus. Moreover, practical, instrumental subjects were included, to train worker activists in communication and organisational skills, with opportunities to gain basic skills in public speaking and debate, in writing and word power, in applied arithmetic, book-keeping and accounts. The inclusion of such courses not only compensated for the inadequacies of formal schooling which, for so many workers, had ended at the age of thirteen or less but, of greater importance, were regarded as vital equipment for service and leadership in the labour movement and socialist cause. Rounded and specialist worker intellectuals were required, for instance, as journalists for the labour and socialist press, as propagandists, as teachers, and as representatives in the wide range of public and political life.

The College would be open for residential, full-time worker students who would attend the core programme of daytime courses. It was intended to spread the College year over three terms, namely, October to December; January to March; and April to June. A programme of three or four months of intensive study was envisaged as the foundation course for each residential student, but with the flexible option of full-time participation for a shorter or longer period. Guidelines, with recommended criteria for the selection of sponsored students were to be issued to labour movement organisations, on the understanding that choice would be based firmly on 'both enthusiasm for knowledge and activity in the workers' movement.'

To fund the College, the December 1915 circular stated that 'the only sound method of financing the scheme would be by the raising of a compulsory levy of one penny a month (say) through the trades organisations.' In the pre-launch period up to 1919, the College committee set a target of £5,000 as the sum required to secure the scheme.[9] It was reckoned that around £2,000 would be required to pilot the College and to cover all costs, including accommodation, staffing, administrative and secretarial expenditure, on the basis of an intake of fifty students in each term. Organisations were asked to provide bursary places worth at least £35 per student, to cover board and lodgings, books, and the course fee of £5.

In addition to the intensive daytime course programme intended principally for the bursary students, a programme of evening and weekend classes was also projected, to be sited on the College premises. However, while this programme was to be based at the centre, a large-scale programme of evening classes was mooted, as an external, outreach effort, with College full-time staff and many part-time tutors and voluntary activists conducting a missionary role, stimulating the formation of classes in local communities throughout the country. The service would be provided for, and in particular aimed at, labour movement organisations which contributed financially and otherwise to the work of the College. Clearly, it was expected that the broad support and major sources of funding for the College base and the ambitious rolling programme of local classes would be forthcoming from the trade union movement, with additional financial support coming from the likes of the co-operative movement and the various socialist organisations.

Expecting the trade union and labour movement to respond with sufficient support, the sub committee, in the December circular, were optimistic that the College would be 'in full swing by October 1916'. However, this forecast was to be rudely dashed by the weight of adverse pressures, particularly during 1916.

The preparatory conference of February 1916 had been a promising start, indicating a wide spread of interest in such a project; but it would require another two large conferences and much additional hard preparatory work besides to convert the principle of support and goodwill into actual material support before the prospect of a College could eventually be realised in 1919–21.

During 1916, government reprisals against labour movement activists on Clydeside removed from the scene several key figures who were playing prominent roles in the promotion of independent working-class education and the Scottish Labour College project. John Maclean, James MacDougall, James Maxton (a keen Labour College supporter) and John Muir were among those imprisoned. Robert Bridges, Arthur MacManus, and Tom Clark were among the Clyde Workers Committee shop stewards to be deported from the area. Moreover, government suppression of the socialist press in Glasgow; the dismantling of the Socialist Labour Party's printing press at the Renfrew Street premises; confiscation of anti-war and revolutionary socialist literature; the enforced cancellation of meetings, exemplified the harsh climate of harassment, censorship and repression which undoubtedly had at least a short-term impact in thwarting the scope for open promotion of advanced political education activity.

Nevertheless, by autumn 1916, Marxist economics and history classes were successfully re-commenced in Glasgow. With Maclean and McDougall in prison, the Central Halls' Sunday classes were taught by J.F. Armour, one of Maclean's longtime political associates, and by Hugh Guthrie, a socialist school teacher. The class, starting with 200 students, ran over the winter until spring 1917.[10] The Glasgow SLP, on its own accord, was also holding large Sunday classes in Renfrew Street and smaller speakers' classes for members.[11]

In early 1917, it was the Glasgow SLP in combination with local Plebs League activists who took the initiative to revive and extend the flagging campaign for independent working-class education. Released from prison in June, Maclean welcomed the move and the declared objective of Plebs activists to co-ordinate and unify the various tendencies in this intensified campaign. In August, he participated in the annual Plebs meeting in London, and supported the joint SLP-Plebs League conference which was planned for September in Glasgow, initiated by the local SLP classes committee. Like the SLC preparatory conferences, this gathering was impressive in the range of delegates represented – the Glasgow District councils of the SLP and BSP; 34 branches of socialist organisations from the SLP, BSP and ILP; the Herald League; the No Conscription Fellowship; 15 'industrial workers groups and workshop committees'; 4 trades councils and 50 trade union branches.[12]

This roll-call of the Left in and around Glasgow agreed to strive for 'the emancipation of the working class' and towards this end, to 'formulate and support Independent Working Class Education, especially economics, industrial history and philosophy'. Despite strongly supported reservations, led by Maclean, that the proposed formation of a Glasgow Plebs League would interfere with and confuse the existing plans and operations of the Scottish Labour College committee, this organisational difference was resolved, the two bodies agreeing to liaise and co-operate with each other in the common purpose 'to secure a chain of Marxist classes in Glasgow and the West of Scotland'.[13]

In the winter of 1917–18, the SLC committee and the SLP-Plebs activists made a significant breakthrough in organising a large programme of Marxist economics and history classes in Glasgow and the West. They did so in the context of a rapidly developing political situation, propelled by the fundamental change in the balance of international class forces resulting from the revolutions in Russia, but also by the renewal of worker militancy in major industrial centres, especially on Clydeside. The ferment on the political left and among advanced sections of workers in the wake of the reception of the October Revolution, the increase of anti-war agitation in 1917 and 1918, and the growing confidence of rank and file trade unionism, notably in engineering and mining, produced a widespread clamour for clarification on a range of crucial issues, including notions of workers' power and control; public and social ownership of the means of production and of essential services; the role of parliament and of extra-parliamentary politics; and the strategy and tactics of workers parties.[14]

One important aspect of, and contribution to, this struggle was an increased interest in and support for the kind of political education which was being promoted and provided by organisations on the left, and by the labour college movement in particular. Here, the phenomenal amount of propagandist work accomplished by John Maclean in this short period was central to the success of the SLC committee. Willie Gallacher, in a remarkable tribute, was sure that 'the work done by Maclean in the winter of 1917–18 has never been equalled by anyone. His educational work would have been sufficient for half a dozen ordinary men, but on top of this he was carrying on a truly terrific propaganda and agitational campaign'.[15] His Central Halls' class had recruited 500 members by November 1917; while the Govan class had 100 members. Maclean conducted another three Marxist classes in Fife, and three in the West; while James MacDougall also taught eight classes in Paisley and in Lanarkshire, mainly in the mining communities where he and rank and file miners were leading the reform movement within the union, demanding workers' control in a socialised industry. In winter 1917, Maclean and MacDougall took all but one of the total of 17 classes organised by the SLC committee, 14 of them in the West of Scotland. The Glasgow Plebs League organised 11 Marxist classes at venues in the city, and also at Dumbarton and Clydebank, where the SLP had branches. Thus the combined effort achieved 27 classes, all in Marxist economics and history.[16]

However, an enhanced class programme was only part of the profile, as the demand for Marxist classes and study groups far exceeded the supply of available tutors. At this stage, the bulk of tutors were worker intellectuals trained by the Socialist Labour Party, and the prominence of Maclean and MacDougall as tutors emphasised the lack of Marxist educators in the Scottish Labour College committee.[17] John McLure, now chairman of the

SLC committee, conducted a Plebs League tutors' class in the summer of 1918, and the SLC committee, through its secretary, J.P. Armour, began to offer a rudimentary correspondence course service for potential groups, sending outline notes, suggestions for reading and advice to leaders of study circles.[18] The committee was also beginning to recruit a bank of tutors from teachers who were 'Socialist MAs', whose services would be required to expand programmes of evening-class work.[19]

However, plans and a timetable agreed at the March 1918 conference for a launch of the day College in the autumn had again to be deferred. While the loss of Maclean's driving energies through another spell of imprisonment between April and November was a severe blow to the campaign, the foremost problem was financial uncertainty, as organisations were slow to respond with substantial donations. All the same, support for the provision of evening and Sunday classes was assuredly growing fast, as shown by the increased size and geographical spread of the class programme in the 1918–19 session. Unfortunately, there is not an exact record of the number of classes which were started and completed in this particular session, but, from the evidence of various press sources, there were at least 20 classes in Glasgow alone, where the Glasgow Plebs League and the SLP were most active. Again, the Central Halls' class was the biggest, followed by the St Mungo Halls' class on the south side, with a combined total of 424 students. The SLC had opened classes in Dumbarton, Paisley, Alexandria and Kilmarnock and had provided speakers and other assistance for study circles at Uddingston, Bellshill, Wishaw, Falkirk and Scotstoun.[20] A Hamilton and District Plebs League was also set up, to augment the existing profile of classes and propaganda in the north Lanarkshire mining communities. In 1918–19, an extensive propaganda campaign had been conducted with ILP branches in Glasgow and Lanarkshire, and the speaking tours of McLure and others had stimulated interest and support for independent working-class education and the College project.

Yet, despite such advances, only a trickle of donations had been received for the College fund by the end of 1918. Admittedly, much political energy and money had been diverted into the general election campaign of late 1918, while the strike struggles of the engineers in the 40 hours' campaign and of the miners in early 1919 would produce further difficulties and distractions. It was already becoming clear that lack of funds was threatening the College as a live proposition. In February 1919, the committee issued a financial appeal to nearly 4,000 organisations. Only £400 out of the target of £5000 had been subscribed by the time of the May conference. Maclean seized the prelude to the conference and its occasion to press the case for the College.[21] At countless public meetings, and in *Forward* and *Worker*, he urged comrades and organisations to renew efforts to fight for support at all levels of the movement, especially in local branches, pit and workshop committees, and in district executive committees. He pointed out the urgency of securing large subscriptions from principal unions such as the miners, and of decisions to levy members at local level when union rule books and official leadership raised obstacles to the funding of external bodies. He exhorted shop stewards to win the approval of their members. Workshop and pit committees could in such cases levy around 1/- a head to send a worker direct from the workplace to a four month scholarship at the day College in September, and thus begin to realise the target of 50 day students, fully sponsored by bursaries and fees. Maclean had returned from a brief spring visit to South Wales where he had witnessed the preparations for examining worker candidates for eight full bursary places at the Central Labour College, the sponsorship being provided by the South Wales Miners Federation.[22]

However, by May 1919, no labour organisations had emulated this example in the West of Scotland and, indeed, none had provided sufficient funding to cover the cost of a student scholarship. Reviewing the sources of donations received before the May conference, Maclean was encouraged by the £10 donations from several co-operative societies and their educational committees, and the likes of the £20 from Cowlairs Co-op; but he was not prepared to accept lame excuses, 'cowardly camouflages', and pleas of poverty from trade unions and branches of socialist organisations who, with a little effort and commitment, could be expected to raise meaningful financial support to accompany their many expressions of goodwill and declarations of support at conferences. In mitigation, he admitted that the committee's financial appeal in the first part of 1919 had unfortunately clashed with the Clyde Defence Committee fund on behalf of the victims of the 40-hour strike and, in solidarity with the jailed comrades and their dependants, they had deliberately allowed that campaign and appeal to take precedence over their own.[23] However, in the middle of 1919, he reckoned that the time of reckoning had come for the labour movement to support the Scottish Labour College scheme and enable the opening of a fully-equipped college, as approved by the May conference.

In two important respects, the outcome of the College launch in the first session of September to December 1919, and January to April 1920 proved a disappointing setback to the original plan, and especially to Maclean. The planned day college courses had to be cancelled, due to the lack of sponsored, full-time students. In December, Maclean declared publicly that 'the main weakness had been the slowness of labour organisations to provide bursaries for students, so as to enable us to commence our day classes – the most important part of our work.' However, he acknowledged the small start in that direction, with a contribution of £50 from the Furnishing trades union.[24]

On the financial front, £1,000 had been collected towards the £5,000 target by December, and the contribution of the miners' unions was largely responsible for that improvement, with the promise of more to come. In early summer, the Midlothian and East Lothian Miners' Association, based at Tranent, had shown the way with a £100 donation. On a recommendation of their executive, the association's 20 branches had voted the money.[25] The West Lothian miners had already funded and appointed a tutor to serve in their area and, after donating £100 in autumn, the Fife, Kinross and Clackmannan Miners' Association also appointed a full-time tutor. Although the Lanarkshire miners were behindhand in this regard, the response to classes was as strong there as in Fife, and by the new year their executive had agreed to award £100. Maclean and MacDougall had high hopes that the Lanarkshire men would soon produce bursary students and at least two full-time tutors to serve their district. In the Ayrshire Miners' Union, a lobby for College grants had narrowly failed to win executive support. At the same time, other organisations were vigorously canvassed.[26]

However, in other respects the profile of the Scottish Labour College in this, its first, 1919–20 session was greatly enhanced.[27] The plan to buy or take out a mortgage on premises had been dropped for financial reasons, but the committee had secured temporary rented premises at the Liberty Rooms, 13 Burnbank Gardens, near St George's Cross. Plebs and SLC activists had already co-operated in holding Marxist economics classes at this socialist educational centre which was also the headquarters of the Glasgow Anarchist Group and Bakunin Press, associated with Guy Aldred.

Here, the College ran a busy and varied evening class programme from Monday to Friday, charging fees of 5/- per subject and 2/6d for every additional subject. John Maclean and William MacLaine, a fellow member of the BSP and former engineering worker who had attended extension classes at Manchester University, were the paid staff tutors. College classes were also held at other venues, often in the premises of labour organisations which supported the work of the College. Apart from Central Halls, where Maclean and John Gready MA lectured in elementary economics and history, advanced economics and constitutional law (labour law and the state) were held in the Women's International League offices, Bath Street, where Helen Crawford, suffragist, anti-war activist and socialist, also a member of the SLC committee, helped to organise enrolment of students for all College evening classes, and advised on course literature.[28]

Partly in order to fill the vacant day programme, the staff tutors offered morning classes on Monday, Friday and Saturday. They were economics and history classes intended for shift workers and night workers, notably miners and musicians, but they did not recruit successfully and the experiment was dropped.[29]

In the 1919–20 session, the SLC programme in Glasgow totalled 30 classes, namely, 15 classes running over two terms of four months, and covering economics, history, English composition, public speaking, mathematics, political science, co-operation, trade unionism, economic geography (imperialism), world revolutions, labour law, shorthand, and Esperanto. Over the two terms, the Glasgow classes enrolled 854 students, 'and the attendance in most of the classes was very satisfactory.'[30]

Outwith Glasgow, 51 classes were recorded in various parts of Scotland, 'with an approximate attendance of 2,000 students.' Successful area conferences had led to the formation of district committees in Aberdeen, Dundee, Edinburgh, Fife, Stirling-shire, Dumbarton, and Ayrshire and they, together with the centrally co-ordinated effort in Glasgow and in Lanarkshire, were responsible for the enlarged programme. In total, four full-time and 21 part-time tutors had conducted classes throughout Scotland, from Aberdeen to Lanark, and although a complete breakdown of class titles and student numbers is not recorded, in the West of Scotland area (excluding Glasgow), classes were held in 19 locations, including 6 in Lanarkshire, 5 in Renfrew, and 3 in Ayrshire. In Glasgow and the West, the Plebs League and the SLC committee formally co-ordinated the engagement of class tutors for the economics and industrial history classes – the principal thrust of the programme, thus making more effective use of their joint tutorial resources.

The Scottish Labour College held its first annual conference in May 1920 in St Andrew's Halls, Glasgow. With 535 delegates representing no less than 335 organisations, it 'was an inspiring sight' and an affirmation of the confidence and spread of interest in education for emancipation. It was an important historic conference but delegates, as ever, were reminded of the dangers of complacency and of the need to build class struggle education into a large movement in order to face the employers' offensive.

In the course of the preceding financial year, constant campaigning among labour organisations had raised a creditable sum of nearly £2,500; and the committee had a balance of around £700 to start the autumn session, to pay for the salaries of two full-time teaching staff and a secretary at the Glasgow centre, as well as for the promotion of further educational work and publicity in the outlying areas.[31]

Conference decided on a constitutional change, cutting the

size of the Scottish committee from 32 to 25 members, and making it a more representative body, firstly on the basis of allocating places to organisations which contributed the most financial support, and secondly, by creating a section with one delegate place from each district committee.

Conference decided to proceed with the day college programme in September, as payments had been received for seven bursary places. The Fife, Kinross and Clackmannan miners' union had voted £450 to cover the cost of three fully-maintained bursary places. The Lanarkshire miners followed suit with £300 and, soon after conference, the Ayrshire miners and the toolmakers' union each contributed funds for one place.

In summer, after selection from their local organisations, prospective bursary candidates from the sponsoring unions sat a written examination to compete for the year-long college places. The eight Scottish students were joined by a Canadian worker, making nine residential students for the first session of 1920–21.

A full day programme was organised, and based at rented premises at 196 St Vincent Street. John Maclean and William McLaine were again engaged as the staff tutors (A.M. Robertson succeeded MacLaine when he left in October). The morning course programme was as follows:

	9–10a.m.	10–11a.m.	11–12	12–12.30p.m.
Mon.	Industrial History	English	Economics	Maths.
Tues.	Political History	Public Speaking	Maths.	Esperanto
Wed.	Industrial History	English	Economics	Esperanto
Thurs.	Political History	Public Speaking	Economic Geography	Esperanto
Fri.	History of Working Class	Evolution	Economics	Maths

This diet of morning classes was followed by afternoon classes in commercial and extra communication subjects. However, this part of the programme was mostly farmed out to the Scottish Business Training College in Bath Street.[32] John MacArthur, one of the miner students from Fife, recollected the exciting, daunting but rewarding experience of an eventful year. He recounted his impressions of Maclean as a charismatic teacher, and singled out the value of his teaching in economics and politics, which enabled the students to gain a broad insight into the labour movement. Occasionally, Maclean took Macarthur and another Fife student John Bird to evening meetings, helping Maclean in his agitational work among the unemployed, chairing the meetings and thus gaining experience in public speaking and organisational skills. He recalled that the students appreciated the economics, politics, history, philosophy and public speaking components, but protested repeatedly about having to take shorthand, bookkeeping, and Esperanto. They doubted the value of such courses, but Maclean insisted, justifying their inclusion as useful skills for labour activists.[33]

It proved to be a troubled year for the College, the greatest disruptions being caused by the course of the class struggle itself. When the miners were locked out in March 1921, all seven miner students decided their real place was back in the coalfield as active participants in the struggle.[34] Moreover, Maclean was unable to conclude his College duties as staff tutor, having again been arrested for political activity, and was in prison between May and August.

From the vantage point of mid-1921, the prospects for a continuation of the day college were extremely bleak, for several reasons. Firstly, no organisations had notified their intention to sponsor bursary places. Secondly, a full prospectus for the coming year had been publicised within the movement, evidently aimed at recruiting a sufficient number of worker students on a non-residential fee-paying basis of £10 for the whole session, or £5 for the half year; but by September this, too, had failed to attract support, and the day college plan was suspended.[35] The failure of this initiative prompted the committee to dismiss the paid services of Maclean, A.M. Robertson and the secretary, Pat Lavin, and at the end of 1921, faced with deteriorating finances, the committee decided to retain only the rented premises at 196 St Vincent Street as an administrative and teaching base for the Glasgow evening class programme.[36]

Powerful economic and financial considerations contributed to this predicament. One critical setback arose from the bankruptcy of the mining unions, following the exhaustion of funds during the employers' lock-out of spring and summer 1921. None of the county unions could afford to contribute fresh bursary places, and this loss of income from the principal supporters of the day college scheme severely damaged and perhaps destroyed the prospect of a revival. However, the reality of hard times for the miners and other trade unions was not a short-term problem, as difficulties in this regard were compounded by the onset of the post-war economic depression from early 1921, worsening during 1922, and bringing heavy unemployment, falling trade union membership and declining funds, especially among the mining, engineering and metal trades unions. In these circumstances, until the temporary economic recovery of late 1923 and 1924, participation in educational classes and schemes came low in the list of priorities among trade unions and their individual members.

However, in reviewing the formative period of the Scottish Labour College project, and attempting to analyse the failure of the residential day college scheme by 1921, it is necessary to enquire further into circumstances and difficulties – other than financial ones – which might have precluded many labour movement organisations and individual workers from making effective and active contributions of support.

Any sober assessment of worker non-involvement as potential or actual day students at the Scottish Labour College has to take account of personal considerations. For many workers who might otherwise have been interested in becoming temporary full-time students, the obstacles and deterrents were probably perceived as being overwhelming, for one or a combination of reasons. Conscious of their lack of formal educational attainments, many must also have lacked the confidence to contemplate – far less tackle – a sustained course of study which involved book learning, written assignments and a formidable new range of subjects and classes in the set curriculum of the day college. John McArthur referred to those problems in his own case, and it was only exceptional political motivation allied to strength

of character which propelled him – as a young militant whose
formal schooling had ended at the age of fourteen – to undertake
the discipline of a rigorous course programme; and moreover,
at the end of the course, face almost certain victimisation from
employment on his return to the coalfield.

Apart from such considerations, the emergence of political
divisions within the Scottish Labour College committee, reflect-
ing differences within the wider labour and socialist movement,
contributed to the defeat and fate of the residential labour
college scheme, as devised by its founders. By 1919 there
was fundamental opposition to the priority, function and role
which John Maclean, in particular, attached to the day college.
Maclean envisaged the Glasgow centre as a teaching school
which, within a short period, and supported by a rising tide of
worker militancy, would turn out tens and perhaps hundreds of
trained class-conscious and revolutionary cadres who would fight
for leadership of the trade union, labour and socialist movement
in the impending decisive battle with capitalism. His explicit
revolutionary perspectives for the day college were rejected by
the majority of the Scottish Labour College committee which, by
1919–20, was already becoming dominated by Labour and ILP
reformist, constitutionalist elements, fronted by the ex-SLPer,
McLure.

Maclean was correct in sensing a conspiracy to block a
revolutionary role for the College and his leading involvement
in its affairs.[37] However, the financial difficulties which beset
the central fund, the limited response to appeals for maintained
bursaries in the first operational year of the residential college,
and the failure to recruit in 1921–22, all served to provide this
opposition element with the pretexts and justifications they
needed to sabotage any continuation of the day college plan.

Opposition and ambivalence were also manifest within the
socialist left on 1920–21, where many former members of the
BSP and SLP who had been closely identified with the College
movement were preoccupied with forming and building the
new Communist Party and, in conditions of political hostility
between them and Maclean, they withdrew active support from
the College as long as he was associated with it. Maclean –

the main driving force behind the College – was becoming increasingly isolated and, for most of 1922, when he was again a political prisoner, was effectively excluded from exerting any real influence on the changing direction of Scottish Labour College affairs.

In essence, a decisive turning point had been reached by 1921. The insurgent mood of labour, particularly in 1917–19, had produced a flush of intense expectation and enquiry for fundamental and revolutionary solutions to the crises of capitalism, war and the emerging post-war society; and one of its manifestations was the extraordinary extent of worker interest in the potential of independent working-class education and Marxist theory which had flourished in the rather chaotic, informal, socialist counter-culture within Glasgow and parts of Clydeside.

However, an outcome of the industrial and political struggles of the immediate post-war years was the defeat of direct action insurgency and the re-shaping of the labour movement, polarised into revolutionary and reformist perspectives, with labour reformism in the ascendancy. This change impacted directly on the course and direction of the Labour College movement and on workers education. 'Independent working class education' could be defended and developed only in so far as the left continued to fight for it politically, with Marxism as the bedrock; but, with the Communist Party appropriating the theory and practice of Marxism and about to transform it into an orthodox doctrine, the continuing existence of 'independent working-class education', as a separate entity, was increasingly vulnerable and exposed.[38] In such conditions it would soon be marginalised, or liable to become the prey of moderating forces in the labour and trade union movement.

By 1922, the formative, heroic and proto-revolutionary phase of the Labour College movement was over, in Scotland and elsewhere in Britain. The residential component of a Scottish Labour College was never to be resurrected, although the programme of district classes continued to expand until 1926.[39] The Scottish Labour College was absorbed into the newly-created National Council of Labour Colleges (NCLC) at the end of 1921. It concentrated on providing an educational scheme and services for nationally affiliated trade unions and depended on gaining official approval.[40] Any remaining Marxist content was soon reduced to rhetoric and, in the post-1926 period, giving way to the Cold War era, it was the paymasters of the NCLC – the leaders of the sponsoring trade unions – who called the tune in terms of the educational provision which they considered to be most appropriate for their members.[41]

NOTES

1. On Maclean, see especially Nan Milton, *John Maclean*, 1973; B.J. Ripley and J. McHugh, *John Maclean*, 1989; Nan Milton ed. *In the Rapids of Revolution*, 1978; D. Howell, *A Lost Left*, 1986 (where Maclean is portrayed alongside James Connolly and John Wheatley).

2. For the Socialist Labour Party on Clydeside and elsewhere, see R. Challinor, *The Origins of British Bolshevism*, 1977. Educational work with a socialist content was, of course, conducted by branches of the Independent Labour Party, and in the many Socialist Sunday Schools in the West of Scotland. However, neither were explicitly marxist in outlook.

3. For an updated guide to the historiography and the debate on Red Clydeside, see Terry Brotherstone 'Does Red Clydeside Really Matter Any More?', in this volume.

4. The origins and early history of the Central Labour College, the Plebs League, and the associated movement for 'independent working class education' are treated in B. Simon, *Education and the Labour Movement 1870–1920*, 1965; John Atkins ed. *Neither Crumbs nor Condescension: The CLC 1909–15*, 1981; and in A. Phillips and T. Putnam, 'Education for Emancipation: The Movement for Independent Working Class Education 1908–1928', in *Capital and Class*, vol. 10, Spring 1980, pp. 18–42. Two accounts by leading figures in the movement are also worth consulting, namely: J.P.M. Millar, *The Labour College Movement*, 1980; and W.W. Craik, *Central Labour College*, 1964. While Atkins, Phillips and Putnam, and Simon address the issue of the extent to which the work of Marx and the theory and practice of marxism were understood and applied by the protagonists of 'independent working class education', the invaluable source for discussion of this issue is Stuart Macintyre, *A Proletarian Science. Marxism in Britain 1917–1933*, 1980, and 1986.

5. The text of the circular is reproduced in Nan Milton, *John Maclean*, pp. 118–9. This biography by Maclean's daughter remains the principal published source of information on the early years of the Scottish Labour College.

6. Milton *ibid*, p. 120.

7. A copy of *A Plea for a Labour College for Scotland* (n.d.) price 2d. is deposited among the records of the National Council of Labour Colleges

Labour College Movement, 1915–1922

(NCLC), in the National Library of Scotland. Accession 5120, Box 6, folio 1. However, the text of the pamphlet is conveniently reproduced in *Milton. Rapids. op. cit.*, pp. 116–122.
8. *Milton. Rapids. op. cit.*
9. Maclean's appeals on behalf of the Scottish Labour College in *Worker*, 10 and 31 May, 1919.
10. *Call*, 14 September, and 12 October, 1916.
11. *Socialist*, July and October 1915; August 1916; June 1917, in 'Glasgow branch report'.
12. *Plebs*, October 1916; December 1916.
13. *Ibid.* September 1917; October 1917 for conference report.
14. The extraordinary upsurge of political enquiry is reflected in, if not confirmed by, the sheer, and probable record amount of meetings and activities called by various groupings on the Left and among workers organisations in Glasgow alone throughout 1918 and into early 1919. Again, it is worth referring to the back page of the weekly *Forward* for the range of meetings. The other socialist newspapers then published in Glasgow, including *Worker*, *Socialist*, *The Spur*, *The Revolution*, also convey the substance of the debates and a sense of urgency of the movement for fundamental change.
15. William Gallacher, *Revolt on the Clyde*, 1936, p. 171.
16. *Plebs*, December 1917 published a synopsis of the classes organised by the Scottish Labour College and Plebs League activists in Scotland.
17. *Plebs*, March 1918. In addition to short reports in *Plebs*, from 1918 until 1924 the fascinating 'public notices' back page of *Forward* – the Glasgow-based ILP weekly paper – is the main source for intimation and details of SLC/Plebs classes in Glasgow and the West of Scotland.
18. *Forward*, 13 April 1918; 1 July 1918.
19. *Plebs*, June 1918.
20. This report, by SLC secretary Willie Leonard, his address and statement to the special conference of the SLC on 24 May, 1919, is in NCLC records, Accession 5120, Additional Papers, Box 20, folio 14.
21. e.g. in *Worker*, 10 and 31 May, 1919.
22. *Worker*, 10 May, 1919.
23. *Ibid*, 17 May, 1919.
24. *Ibid*, 13 December, 1919.
25. See letter from Peter Chambers, president of Midlothian and East Lothian Miners Association (Tranent), in *Worker*, 7 June, 1919.
26. See the 3-page typescript, 'List of Chief Donations from 23rd April 1919 to 31st March 1920', in NCLC records, Accession 5210, Box 6, folio 1.
27. *Report and Proceedings of National Conference of Scottish Labour College*, 29 May, 1920. Provisional Committee of the Scottish Labour College. Published as a 6-page circular, in NCLC records, Accession 5120, Box 6, folio 1.
28. *Forward*, 9 and 16 August 1919.
29. *Ibid*, 20 September 1919.
30. *Report and Proceedings etc. 1920. op. cit.*
31. Willie Leonard's report in *Plebs*, July 1920.
32. The syllabus and timetable is from *Prospectus of the Scottish Labour*

Militant Workers

College (1920–21), in *NCLC* records, Accession 5120, Additional Papers, Box 20, folio 14.

33. See *Militant Miners*, ed. Ian MacDougall, 1981, containing 'The Recollections of John McArthur'; pp. 35–50 deal with his time at the Scottish Labour College.

34. The total programme in session 1920–21 was 30 evening classes in Glasgow and a further 69 classes in the various Scottish districts. *Plebs*, July 1921.

35. Single-page circular, headed 'Scottish Labour College. Students Bursaries' for session 1921–22, signed by P. Lavin, secretary, in NCLC records, Accession 5120, Box 6, folio 2.

36. J.H. Roberts, 'The National Council of Labour Colleges; An experiment in Workers Education: a study of the growth of Labour Colleges with special reference to Independent Working Class Education in Scotland'. M.Sc. dissertation, Edinburgh University 1970, ch. 3, p. 59; also the report by J.P.M. Millar, on the problems and future prospects of the Labour College movement, in 'Scotland's Next Step', *Plebs*, July 1921.

37. Maclean writing in *Vanguard*, July 1920; also comment in Tom Bell, *John Maclean: A Fighter for Freedom, op. cit.*, p. 138.

38. On relations between the Labour College movement and the Communist Party over rival concepts of workers education, see *McIntyre op. cit.; Phillips and Putnam op. cit.*, and A. Miles, 'Workers Education: The Communist Party and the Plebs League in the 1920s', *History Workshop*. no. 18, Autumn 1984. Brian Simon presents a stimulating overview in Simon ed. *The Search for Enlightenment. The Working Class and Adult Education in the Twentieth Century*, 1990, ch. 1, 'The Struggle for Hegemony 1920–26', pp. 15–70.

39. Labour College classes in Scotland: summary totals:

Year	No. of Classes	Student enrolments
1922–23	84	2800
1923–24	152	3928
1924–25	224	5976 (est.)

From 1921, the class programme was organised in nine districts, based on Glasgow, Greenock, Lanarkshire, Ayrshire, Stirlingshire, Edinburgh, Fife, Dundee and Aberdeen.

40. Led by J.P.M. Millar, the first and only general secretary of the National Council of Labour Colleges, the turn to a formal relationship with individual trade unions and with the TUC and STUC dates from 1921, and was largely dictated by the formation of the rival Workers Educational Trade Union Committee (WETUC) in 1919. The WETUC scheme, organised by the (non-Marxist) Workers Educational Association, sought to provide educational facilities for trade unionists. In the early 1920s it had begun to make inroads into trade union education in central Scotland, running classes in economics, history and current affairs, and forming industrial branches. For a general account of this development, see A.J. Corfield, *Epoch in Workers Education*, 1969; and the partisan account by J.P.M. Millar *op.cit.* p. 54.ff.

41. The best treatment of the later history of the NCLC is in the three essay contributions by John McIlroy in Simon, ed., *The Search for Enlightenment. op.cit.* However, the activities of the NCLC and of the WEA in Scotland still require to be fully investigated by historians.

128

CHAPTER 7
Combating the Left: Victimisation and Anti-Labour Activities on Clydeside, 1900–1939

Arthur McIvor and Hugh Paterson

I

Throughout his active political life Harry McShane operated, as did other Marxists and socialists in Scotland, in a hostile environment, suffering discrimination, victimisation and opposition from many quarters. Labour historians have tended to avoid this unsavoury terrain. Hence, the serious breach of civil liberties – noted by Sylvia Scaffardi, secretary of the National Council of Civil Liberties – which those on the left experienced has remained obscured and the work of numerous anti-socialist organisations shrouded in mystery.[1] Recently, the operations of the most vigorous contemporary anti-socialist political blacklisting agency in Britain, the Economic League, have been exposed by investigative journalists both in the press and on television. Direct evidence of a spy network and of blacklisting and victimisation of individuals for their alleged political beliefs – even membership of Anti-Apartheid – has emerged and been cited by newspapers, whilst League officials have been secretly videotaped openly admitting their political vetting role and that they receive, illegally, information on individuals directly from members of the police. The seven regions of the League (including Scotland) are supported by over 2,000 subscribing companies generating an annual budget of over £1 million which is utilised in the dissemination of propaganda and servicing the political blacklist, alleged to include over 50,000 names. The public exposure of such activities led to the Home Secretary appointing an official police enquiry in 1987. Its results, not surprisingly, were inconclusive.[2]

From its origins, the Communist Party on Clydeside suffered from this kind of obstructionism. Several years ago an ex-trade union official realised on applying for a personnel relations job that he was being asked to spy for the Glasgow office of the Economic League! Bob Horne, CP organiser in the Glasgow District Office in the 1940s and early 1950s, recalled how agents of Special Branch MI5 penetrated the CP in Scotland, through phone-tapping, interference with the post, break-ins (to view files) and information passed by *agents provocateurs*, notably Albert Fava. Later, whilst working at George Wimpey, building contractors, as a clerk, Horne discovered that the company operated not one but two blacklists. One was of their own devising – it comprised hooligan elements. The other was supplied by the Economic League.[3]

However, such 'dirty tricks' are not a recent or even a post-1945 cold war era phenomena. Victimisation of those on the left of the political spectrum has a very long history indeed. The aim of this short essay is to explore the mechanisms of such victimisation and other related anti-labour activities in West Scotland over the period 1900–1939.

I

To openly profess one's socialist or communist beliefs in Scotland was extremely risky. Referring to the period immediately prior to the First World War Harry McShane recalled:

> The socialists were always the first to be paid off. In a place like Howden's there would be six or nine months work followed by a slack period. The foreman used to go around quietly on a Friday night to the men he was going to pay off. We watched him: each man would keep his back turned, hoping he would pass by, but the men he stopped at were the ILP members and the other socialists. They were good skilled workers and when trade was busy they would be taken on again; but at the next pay-off it would be they who went first again.[4]

According to his biographers, the Glasgow Marxist Willie Nairn was victimised at least seven times during his tragically short working life up to 1902.[5] John MacLean (a teacher by profession) and his friend James MacDougall (a clerk at the Pollokshaws branch of the Clydesdale bank) were both sacked because of their political beliefs in this period. In MacDougall's case the employers were quite explicit in citing their fears about his agitation and wanted to nip in the bud any possibility of a branch of the Clerks' Union being created in the bank.[6] Willie Gallacher, then a member of the British Socialist Party, experienced great difficulty getting a job after imprisonment for his part in the January 1919 Forty Hours' strike. When a foreman did eventually take Gallacher on, both he and Gallacher were sacked after a week when higher management discovered who they had in their midst![7]

The degree and nature of job discrimination and vetting varied significantly between and within industries, and even within companies, not least because of the very high degree of autonomy which foremen exercised in such matters in this period. However, evidence does suggest that Clydeside employers were amongst the most autocratic and anti-union of British capitalists.[8] Selective re-employment – weeding out activists – after a dispute was common practice, as was the blacklisting of workers on strike to ensure that they were deprived of alternative employment in the region. Professional strikebreakers and 'free labour' agencies were also on hand to provide substitute labour during disputes, as, for example, at Ardrossan in 1910–11.[9] Where employers were also landlords they could utilise the additional leverage of eviction from company housing. A biased judiciary also stacked the cards further against those actively involved in strikes. The Scots miners' leader, Robert Smillie, raised this issue in a letter to the Secretary of State for Home Affairs in November 1898:

> In almost every case either of a strike or lock-out there are a number of prosecutions either for assault or intimidation and the sentences against the men have been very severe. An offence which under ordinary circumstances is met with 10–14 days imprisonment is at the time of a strike punished with six months without any option of a fine. We think the law in this respect needs amendment.[10]

Skilled workers (with the advantage of labour scarcity) and their unions were often treated with more respect by Clydeside employers. However, before 1914, when trade unions were still only just obtaining a foothold in most lesser skilled and female dominated sectors on the Clyde, joining a trade union and involvement in strike action could be enough to precipitate dismissal. J.P. Coats, the Paisley thread manufacturers, discriminated in this way against members of the Amalgamated Society of Dyers in the summer of 1912.[11] Jeannie McKinlay was sacked after six years' service from her job at the Kirtonfield Bleachworks in 1910 because of her courageous attempts to recruit women into the National Federation of Women Workers.[12] Elsewhere, workers were arbitrarily dismissed by autocratic employers who resented any criticism of their working conditions. In February 1911, the manager of a small clothing sweatshop on Argyle St Glasgow (employing 20 women making mantles and shawls and part-owned by a Glasgow Town Councillor, Ballie Mason) sacked a worker who they suspected of providing information to the NFWW (who informed the Factory Inspector) about illegal deductions from earnings. Several years earlier this same woman had been involved in forming one of the first female unions in the Glasgow clothing trade.[13]

The railway companies, coalowners, engineering companies and shipbuilders on Clydeside all developed sophisticated victimisation procedures before World War One, coordinated by their employers' associations. The Lanarkshire Coalmasters' Association operated what they termed 'the block' on striking miners. Similarly, the Engineering Employers' Federation and the Clyde Shipbuilders' Association routinely circulated lists of striking workers to all member firms and enforced, through its rules, the use of the 'enquiry' system to vet applicants for jobs. Railway companies routinely utilised the pretext of breaches of the health and safety 'rule book' to sack union activists, and, in some cases, even union members. Some railway workers emigrated to Australia and South America in an attempt to escape the blacklist.[14] Complaints from unions, reports in the labour press, the use of aliases by victimised activists and the outpayments under victimisation pay of many unions (for example the National Union of Railwaymen) suggest that such blacklisting activities were widespread and could be effective. However, one suspects that much depended on the state of labour markets and the extent to which individual employers within a given industry and region were organised, and hence directly involved in this formalised victimisation network. Significantly, perhaps, we have only unearthed one case prior to World War One on the Clyde where such insidious methods were successfully challenged by the unions. This was when 120 smiths and hammermen struck work at the Hyde Park Locomotive Works in Springburn and forced management to reinstate six hammermen who had been sacked after a week's employment upon the discovery by their manager that they were strikers involved in a long-running wage dispute in Kilmarnock.[15]

In the strife-torn Scottish coalfields, blacklisting and victimisation remained a feature of industrial relations right through to World War Two. 'The older miners', Bob Selkirk recalled, 'had a real dread of victimisation'. One miner was sacked for standing against a coalowner in a parish council election. He subsequently made his peace with the management, became a gaffer and a fervent anti-unionist. Minor legal infringements, usually allowed to pass by management, were a common pretext to weed out undesirable militant workers in the Lothians and Fife. Hence, Russell, a militant justiceman (checkweighman) was summoned to the Edinburgh Sheriff Court, convicted of stealing timber – even though it had been customary for the miners to take home offcuts from the props – and removed from his job. Another miner, at the Smeaton Colliery, was sacked on the pretext of 'impeding production'. Selkirk and his whole section were sacked after initiating a strike at the Ormiston Coal Company when the company refused to pay extra for sorting out small coal in 1909. As elsewhere, the Lothian coalmasters circulated blacklists of all sacked activists to all pits in the region. According to Selkirk, some union agents even passed names to management identifying agitators and recommending they be refused work.[16]

Perhaps the most notorious individual example of political

victimisation on the Clyde prior to World War One occurred at the Singer Sewing Machine Company in Clydebank in 1911. Here, in a renowned anti-unionist multi-national company, the Socialist Labour Party had successfully gained a foothold for their industrial union, the Sewing Machine Workers' Union (affiliated to the Industrial Workers of Great Britain). However, the first all-out strike at the Kilbowie plant in March–April 1911 was countered by mass sackings of between 400 and 1,000 workers, depending on various recorded estimates. Those dismissed included the whole of the almost 200-strong Strike Committee. Workers were asked after the strike if they endorsed the aims of the IWGB and those replying in the affirmative were sacked. Foremen identified and dismissed other workers seen participating at IWGB meetings in Clydebank. Victimisation had occured at Singer before, but the spring 1911 sackings, according to *Forward*, amounted to 'victimisation on such a scale as we have never before had to face'. Questions by Labour members in the House of Commons and an official labour movement boycott of Singer products failed to have any ameliorative effect.[17]

Because many of the sacked activists at Singer were also political activists, this purging had a marked adverse effect on radical socialist politics in Clydebank. Sackings included 60 members of the Independent Labour Party, an undetermined number of Social Democratic Federation members and 22 members of the Socialist Labour Party. The SLP were forced to give up their hall and by the end of the year both the SDF and SLP branches in Clydebank were defunct. The SLP secretary, R. Fleming, noted ruefully:

> That the branch has been hard hit by the action of the Singer company would be folly to deny . . . Members . . . have been practically all cleared out and scattered almost all over the world. Some are still resident in the district, although they travel to various places to dispose of their labour power. When the reaction set in, as was inevitable after such an event as the Singer strike, some of our members lapsed into a sort of apathy.[18]

Attempts to subsequently revive the branch by drafting in some

Jean Rae, c. 1910, actively involved in the Singer strike of 1911; sacked and victimised thereafter (Courtesy of Norma Rae).

of the big guns of the SLP failed. Whilst this undoubtedly satisfied Singer, in a broader sense such a dispersal strategy had positive implications for socialist politics on Clydeside during the subsequent decade. As one SLP member and participant in the Singer strike noted in his autobiography: 'The war was to reveal in the Clyde Workers Committee movement, shop stewards in factory after factory who had once been in Singers'.[19]

Quite apart from such blatant job discrimination socialists on the Clyde prior to 1914 experienced other modes of hostility and opposition. During the sharp trade recessions of 1904–5 and 1908–10 the delinquent fringe of the Orange order campaigned vigorously and violently against socialist meetings. In 1905, William Paul and Neil MacLean of the Socialist Labour Party were arrested when they declined to abandon a meeting which coincided with an Orange demonstration in Bridgeton. MacLean and Paul unsuccessfully pleaded that as the Orange Order had deliberately arranged the clash they should be penalised. In September 1908, violence erupted at an SLP meeting but was contained by the concerted action of Clarion scouts, ILPers, SDPers and SLP supporters. The incident was described in the SLP paper *The Socialist* thus:

> During McLure's address the hooligans attempted to rush the meeting but failed. A ring of stalwarts gripping each others hands proved an unbreakable barrier . . . When the meeting closed down, the hooligans attempted to separate the band of socialists, but failed. The socialists formed themselves into ranks and marched from Bridgeton, amidst the cheers of the workers. . . . The march ended at Jail Square, where comrades Clark and Paul made stirring speeches on the necessity of free speech.[20]

Over the subsequent week meeting after meeting was disrupted and on 6 October the Orangemen, carrying lead pipes and clubs, caught a relatively small, vulnerable group of socialists at a meeting at Whiteinch. *The Socialist* again:

> Only a few hundred socialists turned up. They marched to the street of meeting and were met by a mob of the most brutal ruffians ever organised . . . Numerous accidents happened. One unfortunate socialist was rushed up a stair and there almost killed.

Many workers of the movement received wounds that they will carry for some time. Any speaker who was the least prominent was torn from his comrades and kicked out of the district. Comrade Myers of the SLP was injured and Comrade Paul was surrounded by a crowd who might have sent him to a premature death had not the police collared him.[21]

Significantly, the prior SLP requests for adequate police protection were met by the allocation of just six coppers to cover the meeting! Orange disruption of socialist gatherings continued into the 1920s and 1930s, with, for example, the notorious 'Billy Boys' especially active in the Glasgow East End. On one occasion a prominent Orangeman, Ephraim Connor, was identified trying to infiltrate and spy on a CP meeting, and was found to have a revolver in his pocket![22]

II

The period from the outbreak of war in 1914 witnessed a marked surge in socialist, syndicalist and revolutionary communist ideology. The scenario has been sketched in detail elsewhere: a rising vote for the ILP and the Labour Party, which in 1918 adopted its infamous socialist constitution, together with clause four; rapidly accelerating trade-union membership, from 4 million in 1914 to 8 million members in Britain by 1920, representing a leap from 25 per cent to almost 50 per cent of the total labour force. More alarming to the establishment was the emergence of a synicalist inspired rank and file shop stewards' movement which undermined the bureaucratic controls exercised by the official union leadership and pressed a campaign of extending workers' control deep into the terrain of managerial prerogatives. Moreover, the Bolshevik Revolution in Russia in October 1917 generated mass popular sympathy within Britain, indicated perhaps most starkly in the 'Hands off Russia' movement. The immediate post-war period witnessed unprecedented industrial militancy, coordinated in many areas by the shop stewards, mutinies in the army and navy, strikes of policemen, and vociferous demands for nationalisation of industry, most notably coal mining. Perhaps the forward movement culminated in the winter of 1920–21, at the turning point between post-war replacement boom and the intense inter-war recession, when the Communist Party of Great Britain (which Harry McShane joined in 1922, though his friend John Maclean remained aloof) was formally inaugurated.

The view that this period constituted a potentially revolutionary situation in Britain has now been discredited. However, the evidence does clearly suggest that the immediate post-war years did witness the culmination of a profound challenge to the ideological hegemony of capitalism in Britain. 'Crucially', Stephen White has noted, 'the legitimacy of bourgeois norms and political institutions was contested. Respect for Parliamentary government rapidly declined; and radical categories of economic analysis gained an increasingly wide currency.'[23] How the threat from labour was perceived is perhaps more important than objective reality. The events of 1919–20 certainly caused widespread alarm amongst the British Establishment. The Prime Minister, Lloyd George, perceived what he termed 'the spectre of a soviet republic' during the labour unrest of 1919, and a year later the government's chief industrial conciliator, George Askwith, commented: 'Propaganda ceaselessly presses for a change of social life, a better position for the workers, and more control'.[24] In a more paranoic vein were the influential fortnightly reports to the Home Office of Basil Thomson, head of the Special Branch, Scotland Yard, on 'Revolutionary Organisations in Britain', which included alarmist surveys of revolutionary socialist activities on the Clyde.

Employers and the state responded in a number of ways to the escalating threat to capitalist hegemony. The Lloyd George Cabinet consolidated its strikebreaking machinery and secretly sponsored a pro-constitutional propaganda agency run by Sidney Walton. Many employers, especially those in the newer industries, openly courted class reconciliation, fervently embraced union recognition and collective bargaining in an attempt to impose procedural controls and institutional constraints over labour – to muzzle spontaneous industrial militancy. Other capitalists sought to extend their control over the labour process by introducing new technology, extending scientific management techniques popularised in America, thus intensifying the division of labour and displacing pivotal and militant craftsmen. Employer paternalism was also extended – as at ICI and Singer, Clydebank, for example – taking the form of sophisticated, bureaucratised welfare and recreation schemes, designed to defuse labour militancy, increase efficiency and retain loyalty to the firm.

However, a common defensive response of employers in this period was to band together – to defend their interests through combination. Hence, existing collective organisations of employers were strengthened and new alliances forged. Pressurised by labour, individual employers increasingly affiliated to the industry-wide employers' associations, whose total number in Britain increased over 1914–25 from 1,500 to 2,400. The first durable employers' federations also emerged over this period, the Federation of British Industries (FBI) in 1916 and the National Confederation of Employers' Organisations (NCEO) in 1919. Concurrently, a number of other employers' organisations were established with more overt anti-labour and anti-bolshevik objectives, including the British Empire Union (1916), the Middle Class Union (1919), the Reconstruction Society and the Economic League.

Contrary to the revisionism of recent writers like Ian McLean and Christopher Harvie, Clydeside workers did play a vanguard role in the socialist movement in this period and did exhibit unequivocal signs of a heightened class consciousness, perhaps more so than any other industrial area in Britain. What Morris, Melling and others have recently demonstrated is that the concept of Red Clydeside still retains much of its validity, even if it is accepted that Willie Gallacher's prognosis of a Petrograd on the Clyde is an exaggerated distortion of reality.[25] Evidence suggests that the intensity of this threat to Clydeside capital over the turbulent years from 1910 through to the mid-1920s generated a radical, coercive reaction. In the engineering sector the termination of hostilities and the fall in demand for munitions provided the first opportunity to weed out militant shop stewards from the shop floor. The sharp recession of 1921–2, massive growth in unemployment levels and the successful prosecution of the pivotal industry-wide lock-out in British engineering in 1922 provided further opportunities for Clydeside employers to victimise activists. So too did the General Strike of 1926, as Ian McDougall has shown. Glasgow tramway workers and printers at the *Glasgow Herald* and the *Evening Times* were amongst those sacked after the General Strike.[26] Members of the Railway Clerks' Association in Glasgow were only reinstated if they agreed to sign a statement that they were returning 'unconditionally' after the General Strike.[27]

Mick McGahey's father, who worked in a coal mine in Shotts, was sacked at this time and the family were forced to move down to Kent, where McGahey found work in the atrociously wet Kent coal pits. Bob Selkirk was sacked from the Kirkford pit in 1920 after writing a vitriolic letter to the Glasgow *Evening Times* exposing the criminal lack of ventilation in the pit. Despite obtaining promises of employment at several pits thereafter, Selkirk recalled, 'the Head Office ban prevented me actually working.'[28] After several sackings between 1920 and 1924 Selkirk became Fife organiser for the National Unemployed Workers' Movement.

In the Vale of Leven, retrenchment at the United Turkey Red Company provided the backdrop for a vicious management attack on the labour activists in their employ, particularly the communists in the early and mid-1920s. Sackings forced many to migrate from the area to seek work, whilst those who remained often experienced dire problems obtaining alternative employment. Stuart Macintyre notes:

> The irreplaceable Dan O'Hare had to be set up with a horse and float to sell vegetables: David McKim earned a living with his brother as a photographer; Hugh Macintyre was identified and sacked after a few weeks at Singers in Clydebank and he eventually became an insurance agent. Since it was generally sufficient for a dyehand to be seen at a Communist meeting to be thrown out of work, the Communist Party lacked any base in the dyeing and printing industry. . . . By 1925 there was not a single factory group of Communists left in the Vale. . . . by the end of the decade only two were employed.[29]

Dan O'Hare asserted bitterly that the Communist Party Executive developed no effective strategy in response to such victimisation. But what could they have done? By the early 1930s, according to the rather overstated prognosis of the communist author, Allen Hutt, the shop stewards' movement had atrophied in West Scotland because the depression had facilitated a process whereby the most active elements had been forcibly removed from the workplace. 'A trip along the Clyde today', Hutt noted in 1933, 'is like visiting a cemetery'.[30]

Clydeside employers sought to close ranks and counter the threat from labour, partly by consolidating their industry-wide employers' organisations and sponsoring the formation of specialist anti-labour propaganda and political vetting agencies. The most influential and powerful of these anti-socialist agencies was the Economic League. Because of its leading role in Clydeside anti-socialist politics in the 1920s and 1930s this organisation merits more detailed scrutiny.

The Economic League was created by a group of extreme right-wing politicians, industrialists and financiers in collaboration with military intelligence specialists in 1920. The initiative came from a Conservative MP (later Party Agent, 1923) Sir Reginald 'Blinker' Hall (1870–1943). Hall had, significantly, been Director of Naval Intelligence at the Admiralty, 1914–18. Convinced of the need to create an anti-subversive organisation as part of a broader 'crusade for capitalism' he invited a number of leading industrialists to a meeting at Westminster. Among those present at the inaugural meeting were representatives of the most powerful employers' federations in Britain, including Sir Allan Smith, director of the Engineering Employers' Federation, Cuthbert Laws, director of the Shipping Federation, and Evan Williams, chairman of the Mining Association. The Economic League was formally constituted with a budget of £50,000 and Hall was made chairman of the new organisation, a position he held until 1924. One of the first jobs of the League was to generate wider support and galvanise employers to create regional committees to explore ways in which socialist and communist influence within working-class communities might be more effectively neutralised.[31]

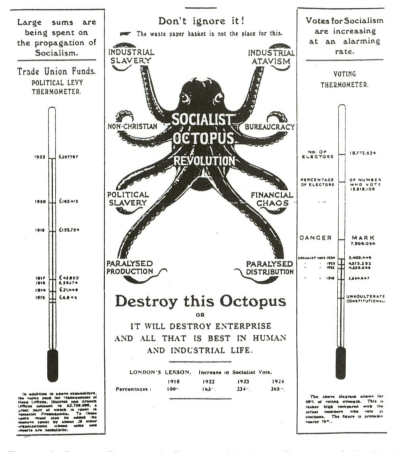

Economic League Propaganda Poster, mid-1920s. (Courtesy of the Trades Union Congress Library)

A Scottish Economic League (SEL), with three affiliated committees in Glasgow, Edinburgh and Dundee, was formed in November 1920, when representatives of two anti-socialist organisations – The British Empire Producers' Organisation and National Propaganda – merged their interests. The *Glasgow Herald* welcomed the development, arguing in October 1921 that recent events 'clearly demonstrated that the communists and extreme revolutionary socialists had taken the fullest advantage of the present industrial crisis to stir up trouble and to exploit the sufferings of the unemployed in favour of revolution.'[32] Not surprisingly the West Scotland branch of the Economic League (WSEL) emerged in the 1920s as the most vigorous of the three Scottish areas. After all, it was operating, as it liked to torridly assert, in 'the Red Capital of the Empire'. The Glasgow based organisation was initially chaired by Lord Glentanar (president) and included J.R. Richmond, Sir Thomas Dunlop, William Brodie, George Barclay, Sir F.C. Gardiner, Sir Alexander Walker and Professor Rait on its Executive Committee in 1921–2. Another prominent EL Central Committee member was the Scottish industrialist, Lord Invernairn (William Weir), who had coordinated the dilution campaign during World War One on the Clyde.[33] The objects of the SEL were defined thus:

To promote on strictly non-political lines the teaching of sound political economy, to foster cooperation between employers and employed and to resist those elements that make for dissension and unconstitutional activities.[34]

Thus the SEL aimed to disseminate knowledge and understanding of classical, orthodox economics, commend individual enterprise and efficiency, defend and champion private ownership and diminish disruptive industrial unrest. The collectivist approach was castigated whilst individualism was praised. A prominent member of the WSEL, Sir John Cargill, noted in 1925: 'All Labourists and Socialists are Idealists. But idealism will never carry on in this world. Self-interest is the mainspring of human nature.'[35] This theme was carried further in a Central League pamphlet published in 1929:

A new world of amazing human contrivances has arisen since the early days of the last century; life is fuller, freer and richer in every way. Private enterprise has quickened the world with a new vitality. Running through the system is a magic spirit, the very spirit of life itself, that indefinable something which, for want of a more scientific definition, is called Individual Initiative and Enterprise'.[36]

As with many radical right-wing organisations there is some mystery surrounding the financial backing enjoyed by the regional Economic Leagues. The major source of support was generated from voluntary subscriptions of sympathetic individuals, companies, banks and employers' associations. Employers' organisations, in particular, sustained the Economic League with substantial donations. The composition of the WSEL would suggest that it was engineering, shipbuilding and coal interests that dominated. No evidence has come to light of the WSEL receiving direct funding from, or subscribing to, any political parties. Indeed, it claimed to stand above party politics and never got involved in local or national elections on Clydeside. This, however, didn't stop representatives of the WSEL speaking regularly to Conservative and Unionist Associations, or openly opposing the minority Labour governments of 1924 and 1929–31. These Labour administrations were particularly attacked for their increased interference in industry and alleged profligate overspending through unemployment dole payments. On the other hand, the Tory dominated National Government from 1931 was fully supported by the WSEL, on the grounds that it had succeeded in 'rescuing the country from the financial morass into which it had been allowed to drift.'[37] The Central League continued to maintain good relations and met regularly with other smaller anti-socialist organisations and at least two of the EL General Council members were linked with the Friends of Nationalist Spain and the Anglo-German Fellowship in the 1930s. The Central Council of the Economic League was also a founder member of the international anti-bolshevik organisation, Entente Against the Third International, created in 1925, and was the British representative on this body through the 1920s and 1930s. Little is known about this intriguing international organisation. However, the position of the Economic League within it perhaps provides some indication of the dominant role the League had achieved within the anti-bolshevik movement in Britain by the mid-1920s.

To a large extent, the methods adopted by the West Scotland Economic League in the 1920s and 1930s directly duplicated those of the left, concentrating on what the League called 'educative propaganda' to get its anti-socialist message across to working people on the street and within working-class communities. Public meetings were arranged wherever a platform could be obtained; in halls, clubs, at street corners, factory gates, market places, parks and outside employment exchanges. On occasions, employers brought in the League to provide a series of lectures for their workpeople as part of the company 'welfare' programme. Moreover, by the 1930s the WSEL were also organising special touring campaigns, using motorised 'flying squads' (apeing the clarion vans) and several speakers to saturate a particular town or region with propaganda. Fife and Dundee, for example, were targeted in this way by the WSEL in 1937.[38] Members of the WSEL deliberately went out into what they regarded as the most radical districts of Glasgow to spread the word, whilst during the Glasgow Fair period, attention was diverted to the coastal holiday resorts, including Rothesay, Largs and Irvine. The WSEL claimed to have held 1,200 individual meetings in the first six months of its existence to May 1921 and to have averaged a little over 1,000 open air meetings per year during the 1920s.[39] However, obviously such internally generated figures — impossible to verify — need to be treated cautiously.

The WSEL organised such activities with military precision. A staff of speakers (initially 12) were recruited and provided with two months' intensive training in economics at a Glasgow college under the direction of a full-time League lecturer, C.H. Temple, who later became WSEL Secretary. Temple created a statistical and information bureau to provide his corps of speakers with the most up-to-date material, including weekly 'notes for speakers' and the 'Hints for Hecklers' produced by the Central Council of the League. To retain the impetus of its propaganda through the winter months the WSEL formed small study circles and groups in 1924 (after the communist factory 'cells') which met regularly to study economics, working to a definate syllabus, with periodic examinations. It was noted by an opponent in *Plebs* in 1927 that this was one way the League popularised 'Boss-Economics'.[40]

There is some evidence to suggest that communists on the Clyde took the Economic League seriously. Helen Crawfurd recalls 'considerable opposition' from the WSEL in her unpublished autobiography.[41] Finlay Hart, Communist Party organiser in West Scotland, remembered Economic League speakers being very able and well briefed when addressing meetings or heckling at works gates around Clydeside and on Glasgow Green in this period.[42] There were, inevitably, outbreaks of violence at such meetings. The Central Council reported examples of its speakers being met by spitting, stone throwing and stink bombs. The WSEL reported in 1921:

> The socialists discovered that the League were conversant with their subject and that they were a force to be reckoned with and from May (1920) we experienced violent, organised opposition and on many occasions platforms were rushed and every possible method employed to prevent the speakers of the League from delivering their message. This opposition was, however, gradually broken down.'[43]

The League backed up the spoken word by writing, printing and disseminating literally millions of leaflets, which were extensively distributed in Britain through the regional Leagues, and mailed to other anti-subversive organisations worldwide by the League's Information and Research Department. Periods when the labour movement achieved a high public profile, such as during the General Strike, 1926, and the Hunger Marches of the 1920s and 1930s, were also phases of unprecedented activity for the regional Economic Leagues. Though no precise details have emerged of the activities of the WSEL during the General Strike, the General Council reported that its affiliated regional Leagues were playing an active role in strikebreaking, encouraging the enrolment of volunteer workers, providing lorry drivers and transporting foodstuffs, publishing news sheets and leaflets attacking 'the pernicious influence of the reds' and propagating the League's new slogan: 'every man is a capitalist'. In the aftermath of the General Strike, the General

Council organised a massive convention in London and openly supported the campaign of the 'hawks' in the Baldwin Cabinet for drastic reforms in British labour law and the introduction of 'contracting-in' to the political levy. This resulted in the passing of the draconian Trade Union and Trade Disputes Act, 1927, known in the labour movement as 'the blacklegs charter'. This measure, according to the president of the West Scotland EL, was essential 'to protect the community from the abuse of power by the trade unions'.[44] In 1932 and 1934 the regional Leagues used their motor propaganda vans to precede the various contingents of hunger marchers along their route, holding meetings and distributing leaflets in towns directly before the hunger marchers arrived. The Central Council of Economic Leagues produced a special pamphlet on the 1934 march in which they exposed it as 'a communist stunt . . . part of the Communist Party policy of causing trouble whenever and wherever possible'. The pamphlet concluded, rather pathetically: 'NUWM may stand for National Unemployed Workers' Movement, but it also stands for *No Use Walking Miles*'.[45] Elsewhere, other methods were used to undermine the Hunger Marches. Bob Selkirk was waylaid by three policemen, two of whom held him fast while the third systematically beat him up. In a bizarre variety of victimisation, the Tory-controlled Fife County Council 'had the married men who marched to London arrested as wife deserters.'[46]

The Economic League also cleverly utilised its educational services as a 'cover' to obscure a more unsavoury strategy; that of ensuring, via a sophisticated centralised blacklist, that all militant socialists, communists and other loosely defined 'subversives' were kept out of employment and hence positions of influence in Britain. The Central Council of Economic Leagues appears to have first organised such a confidential service for employers in 1925 when the chairman, Sir Auckland Geddes, reported that he had initiated 'the compilation of a chart and dossier of socialist and subversive organisations and . . . arrangements are in hand for a permanent clearing house of information in connection with alien organisations and individuals.'[47] Regional Economic Leagues could tap into this blacklist. Whilst the exact constitution and mechanics of the political victimisation service developed by the WSEL remains obscure, evidence shows that by the 1930s subscribing firms were certainly utilising the services of the regional Economic Leagues to vet applicants for work and to identify militants for dismissal. Nor did the League wait for employers to approach them. In 1931, reports on over 150 Young Communist League 'cells' were forwarded to regional Leagues and from them to the 'penetrated' factories.[48] Information on communist activity and names to add to the blacklist came from scrutinising the labour press and through a shady espionage network involving police, paid spies and informants. Wal Hannington noted in *Unemployed Struggles* that the CPGB was crawling with infiltrators and *agents provocateurs*.[49] Harry McShane suggested in his memoirs that disillusioned communists provided information to the League and even named an ex-chairman of the NUWM who, he alleged, offered his services to the Economic League.[50]

Stolen papers from the Manchester office of the Economic League, subsequently cited in a front-page exposé in the communist paper, the *Daily Worker*, in May 1937, widely publicised the previously highly clandestine political vetting service of the League. The published letters indicated quite categorically that both the General Council and the regional Leagues kept card indexes with data on 'subversive' individuals and organisations, noting their movements and activities, and that they used this pool of data to keep companies informed. The *Daily Worker* letters also indicated that the Economic League operated closely with local police forces. League officials met with detectives specialising in subversion, arranged to mutually cover meetings and surveillance, and sent reports to the police of illegalities committed by individuals on the political left. In return, the League were forwarded police reports of communist meetings and allowed access to police files, clearly an illegal action under the Official Secrets Act, 1911. Despite a furore in the House of Commons, such activities were covered-up by the Attorney General, who refused to initiate legal action against the League.[51] Obviously, they had sympathisers in high places!

III

The Economic League provides an example of the knee-jerk reactions of a segment of capital on Clydeside to what was perceived (regardless of objective reality) to be a dire threat to capitalist hegemony. The League's philosophy was based on the premise that control could be maintained and the survival of capitalism ensured only by a comprehensive programme of paternalistic re-education of workers into the basic tenets of orthodox economics and an active policy of discrimination through blacklisting designed to deny 'intractable' militant workers access to employment and hence close contact at the point of production with other workers. This would minimise industrial disruption and prevent the socialist cancer spreading further.

The role of the Economic League needs, however, to be kept within its proper perspective. Its work constituted just one element of a much broader, multi-faceted capitalist counter-attack against labour in the inter-war period. Moreover, victimisation of workers and anti-labour propaganda was not monopolised by this one organisation. The propaganda initiatives of the Economic League in the 1920s owed much to the pre-war work of the Anti-Socialist Union.[52] Foremen, managers and individual employers, on Clydeside, as elsewhere, exercised their power to withold employment to workers on political, as well as religious and ethnic grounds. Nor was such political discrimination and blacklisting confined solely to Britain, or, indeed taken so far in Britain as elsewhere. The international anti-bolshevik organisation, Entente Against the Third International, had affiliates in 15 nations, all of which discussed tactics and exchanged ideas in their periodic meetings through the 1920s and 1930s. In Germany and Italy there existed a long tradition of political victimisation, intensified by the emergence of Fascism. Moreover, in comparison to the anti-labour activities of American capitalists, the work of the Economic League in Scotland was tame. In the late 1930s Leo Huberman brilliantly exposed the way in which American employers utilised the services of detective agencies to infiltrate trade unions and political organisations, provide names and information, and undermine labour militancy. Incredibly, more than 230 separate detective agencies in the USA, including the infamous Pinkertons, Burns and Railway Audit agencies, netted in revenue an estimated $80 million per year in the 1930s for industrial spying, espionage and blacklisting services. The implications of this, as Huberman noted, was that 'the policies of Congress, as declared in the Wagner Act [1935, providing for trade union recognition], are completely defeated by industrial espionage.'[53]

Access to the archives of the Economic League, not surprisingly, has been denied, and without this it is impossible to arrive at any conclusive assessment of its role and effectiveness in West Scotland. On the one hand, it is tempting to dismiss the League as another insignificant, small, 'crank' far-right organisation. Like William Collison's National Free Labour Association before World War One, the Economic League and its affiliated regions almost certainly exaggerated their own importance, and figures cited in printed annual reports and pamphlets for numbers of meetings, study circles and so on need to be treated with extreme caution, as does the claim of the West Scotland Economic League that it was largely responsible for diminishing the influence of revolutionary communism on the Clyde in the 1920s. Indeed, measured against the rising socialist vote in the 1920s, the League's propaganda failed miserably. Scottish workers were rarely taken in by such puerile and obvious attempts at manipulation. The Economic League also failed to prevent the Communist Party revival in the late 1930s when Party membership doubled in four years and CP members were drawn back into employment during the rearmament drive. This was a period when skilled engineers were at a premium in the labour market – on Clydeside and elsewhere – and when the opportunity of making a quick and substantial profit (after such a long dearth of sizeable profit margins) made employers and management less sensitive towards the political affiliations and past experience of job applicants. Bob Selkirk, for example, regained work at the Fife Coal Company in 1938, because rearmament revived demand for coal and the company decided to suspend its boycott of labour activists.[54]

On the other hand, the Economic League provides us with further conclusive evidence of the widespread prevalence of discrimination exercised against those on the left of the political spectrum. Blacklisting is impossible to quantify, though we have enough evidence to strongly suggest that this was endemic. Victimisation of Labour activists, as we've seen, was already an integral part of the fabric of industrial relations on the Clyde before World War One, whilst mass unemployment between the wars enabled such tactics to be easily hidden. From the 1920s, the Economic League played an important part in supplementing, systematising and centralising this process. Indeed, they appear to have been the only organisation in inter-war Britain providing a nation-wide, centralised political blacklisting service of this kind. Moreover, the very durability of the Economic League through to the present bears testimony to its effectiveness as a blacklisting agency. It is inconceivable, surely, that big firms, banking and financial interests, and employers' associations on the Clyde and in other regions would continue to financially support and patronise an organisation like this if it was not providing a satisfactory service.

The Economic League thus provides evidence of the lengths that a strand of particularly autocratic Clydeside employers went to in order to oppose socialist ideas and ensure that the advocates of 'subversive' socialist and Marxist doctrines were kept off the shop floor. Did this have a demoralising impact and successfully cut the lines of communication between the revolutionary socialist movement and those who were fortunate enough to retain their jobs during the depression? Possibly so – at least up to the mid-1930s. More evidence needs to be gathered to verify this hypothesis. Victimisation may also have worked to further sharpen class consciousness amongst those being discriminated against, thus incubating trouble for the future. Moreover, by forcibly exorcising the 'problem' from the shop floor, capitalists inadvertently contributed to strengthening the influence of socialist and communist ideas amongst the unemployed. Sacked and laid-off activists diverted their energies to struggle within the community and campaigning within the National Unemployed Workers' Movement. Victimisation clearly constituted a serious breach of workers' civil liberties, compounded, the evidence indicates, by the explicit and illegal support of the police and the implicit connivance of the State in this action. The chronicle of such insidious practices from the turn of the century to World War Two brings into very sharp focus the considerable risks and sacrifices that committed socialists and communists were forced to endure on Clydeside and elsewhere.

NOTES

We would like gratefully to acknowledge the many helpful comments of Rob Duncan, generous aid locating sources from Audrey Canning at the Gallacher Library, and Bob Horne and the late Finlay Hart for providing interviews. Our work has also benefited considerably from the criticisms, ideas and comments of the Glasgow Labour History Workshop.

1. See S. Scaffardi, *Fire Under the Carpet* (1986)
2. For example, see Granada TV, *World In Action*, 1 Feb. 1988; *The Guardian*, 19 March 1987; *Morning Star*, 19 Nov. 1988.
3. *Oral interview*, Hugh Paterson with Bob Horne (21 August 1990)
4. H. McShane and J. Smith, *No Mean Fighter* (1978), pp. 19–20. See also pp. 8–9; 31, 44.
5. H. Savage and L. Forster, *All for the Cause: Willie Nairn 1856–1902* (1991), pp.
6. *Forward*, 13 March 1909; 20 March 1909; 27 March 1909. We are grateful to Irene Sweeney for this reference.
7. W. Gallacher, *Revolt on the Clyde* (1936), pp. 248–9.
8. See A. Reid, 'Employers' Strategies and Craft Production', in S. Tolliday and J. Zeitlin (eds.), *The Power to Manage? Employers and Industrial Relations in Comparative Perspective* (1991), p. 38; J. Melling, 'Scottish Industrialists and the Changing Character of Class Relations in the Clyde Region, c.1880–1918', in T. Dickson (ed.), *Capital and Class in Scotland* (1982).
9. On Ardrossan, see B. Kenefick (BA Dissertation, History Dept, University of Strathclyde, 1991). For a more detailed discussion of blackleg importation during British strikes see A.J. McIvor, 'Employers' Organisation and Strikebreaking in Britain, 1880–1914', *International Review of Social History*, XXIX (1984).
10. Correspondence, 29 November 1898 filed in Public Record Office (Kew, London), HO 45/9930/B25921.
11. *Forward*, 3 August 1912, p. 7.
12. *Forward*, 20 August 1910; *Glasgow Herald*, 6 September 1910
13. *Forward*, 4 February, 1911
14. P. Bagwell, *The Railwaymen* (1963), pp. 194–5.

Victimisation and Anti-Labour Activities, 1900–1939

15. From Glasgow Labour History Workshop, unpublished notes on Clydeside strikes, 1910–14
16. Bob Selkirk, *The Life of a Worker* (1967), pp. 7–9.
17. For a detailed examination of this incident see, Glasgow Labour History Workshop, *The Singer Strike, Clydebank, 1911* (1989).
18. *The Socialist*, December 1911.
19. Tom Bell, *Pioneering Days* (1941), p. 75.
20. Cited in D. Unger, *The Roots of Red Clydeside* (Ph.D. thesis, University of Texas, 1979), pp. 329–32, where these events are dealt with in more detail.
21. *Ibid.*
22. McShane and Smith, *op. cit.*, pp. 124–5. See also pp. 143, 205–6.
23. S. White, 'Ideological Hegemony and Political Control: The Sociology of Anti-Bolshevism in Britain, 1918–20' *Scottish Labour History Society Journal*, 9, 1975, p. 3.
24. G.R. Askwith, *Industrial Problems and Disputes* (1920), p. 486; K.O. Morgan (ed), *Lloyd George: Family Letters, 1885–1936* (1973), p. 190. See also T. Jones, *Whitehall Diary, vol. 1, 1916–25*, edited by Keith Middlemas (1969), pp. 96–103.
25. For references to this debate and a full discussion see chapter 3 by Terry Brotherstone.
26. I. MacDougall, 'The General Strike in Scotland' in I. MacDougall (ed), *Essays in Scottish Labour History* (1978), pp. 195–7. See also I. MacDougall (ed), *Militant Miners: Recollections of John McArthur* (1981), pp. 110–17.
27. P. Bagwell, *op. cit.*, p. 486.
28. B. Selkirk, *op. cit.*, p. 13.
29. S. Macintyre, *Little Moscows* (1980), p. 99. For a recurrence in 1934 at the UTR see Macintyre, pp. 102–3.
30. A. Hutt, *The Condition of the Working Class in Britain* (1933), p. 98. For a more balanced assessment see E. Lancaster, 'Shop Stewards in Scotland: The Amalgamated Engineering Union Between the Wars', *Scottish Labour History Society Journal*, 21, 1986, pp. 26–33; and A. McKinlay, 'Depression and Rank and File Activity: The AEU, 1919–1939', *Scottish Labour History Society Journal*, 22, 1987, pp. 22–29.
31. For a more detailed investigation of the work of the Economic League in Britain between the wars see A.J. McIvor, 'Political Blacklisting and Anti-Socialist Activity between the Wars', *Bulletin of the Society for the Study of Labour History*, 53, 1 (Spring 1988). For a broader context see M. Hollingsworth and R. Norton-Taylor, *Blacklist* (1988).
32. *Glasgow Herald*, 14 October 1921.
33. A. Hutt, *op. cit.*, pp. 101
34. *Glasgow Herald*, 19 October 1921.
35. *Ibid.*, 8 April 1925.
36. Economic League, *The Facts About Industry* (1929), pp. 3–4
37. *Glasgow Herald*, 19 May 1932.
38. *Ibid.*, 9 March 1937.
39. *Ibid.*, 19 May 1931.
40. *Plebs*, October 1927; *Glasgow Herald*, 8 April 1924.
41. H. Crawfurd, unpublished autobiography, held in the Marx Memorial

Library, London, p. 155. We are grateful to Audrey Canning for this reference.

42. Oral Interview, Arthur McIvor with Finlay Hart, Glasgow 25 May 1985.

43. West Scotland Economic League, *Report*, cited in the *Glasgow Herald*, 19 October 1921.

44. *Glasgow Herald*, 30 April 1927.

45. Economic League, *Counter-Communist Campaign* (pamphlet, 1934), pp. 2–6.

46. B. Selkirk, *op. cit.*, p. 29.

47. Cited in 'The Economic League', *State Research Bulletin*, 7, August–September 1978, p. 138.

48. Economic League, *Annual Report* (1931), p. 9; *Annual Report* (1932), pp. 13–14.

49. Wal Hannington, *Unemployed Struggles, 1919–1936* (1936) pp. 141–53.

50. H. McShane and J. Smith, *op. cit.*, p. 219.

51. *Daily Worker*, 8 May 1937; 10 May 1937; *The Times*, 12 June 1937; 15 June 1937 and 22 June 1937; *Economic League Bulletin*, 27 June 1937.

52. See K.D. Brown, 'The Anti-Socialist Union, 1908–1949', in K.D. Brown (ed), *Essays in Anti-Labour History* (1974), pp. 234–61.

53. See Leo Huberman, *The Labor Spy Racket* (1938). For a fascinating biography of Pearl L. Bergoff, the leading US strikebreaker between 1910 and the mid-1930s, see E. Levinson, *I Break Strikes!* (1935).

54. B. Selkirk, *op. cit.*, p. 13.

CHAPTER 8

James Connolly, James Larkin and John Maclean: the Easter Rising and Clydeside Socialism

James D. Young

Connolly has been mythologized by post-1916 Irish nationalism and by post-1917 Soviet Marxism as, respectively, the socialist who made a stand for the Irish nation and the Irish Lenin who acted on the Leninist principle of the right of nations to self-determination. Both myths cross-fertilize, the former eliding the socialist critique of Connolly's politics and the latter distorting his real contribution to international socialism. There was but one Connolly, but he drew on the separate traditions of Second International Marxism and Irish nationalism.

—*Austen Morgan*

The name of John Maclean will live along with James Connolly and Lenin when the imperialist lackeys of Stormont are as a forgotten sound. It was Lenin who said that the Irish fighter and the Scotsman had the correct approach to the war of 1914–18.

—*Mary Brooksbank*

In suggesting that an unbroken friendship between James Connolly and John Maclean began in 1903, Nan Milton was reinforcing established myths about the major prefigurative Irish and Scottish 'Leninists' during the early phase of the First World War. In fact, Connolly and Maclean never met or corresponded, though Maclean and James Larkin met and formed a close and enduring friendship in 1907.[1] Moreover, Maclean did not acknowledge Connolly's so-called authentic Leninist precocity before 1922. As Nan Milton puts it: 'In 1922 Maclean was to declare "when Jim Connolly saw how things

155

were going on the Clyde, he determined on the Easter Rising".'[2] Far from James Connolly, James Larkin or John Maclean being Leninists, they were Marxian socialist-humanists who were not entirely irreligious.

The Scottish branches of the British Socialist Party and the De Leonist Socialist Labour Party were not sympathetic towards the Easter Rising – at least not in 1916. Despite the undocumented and unsubstantiated romantic myths to the contrary, Scottish socialists did not engage in gun-running to Ireland in 1915 or 1916.[3] But just as John Maclean eventually attributed the Easter Rising to the inspiration James Connolly derived from the anti-war agitation on Red Clydeside, so Walter Bell ultimately invented a myth about the Socialist Labour Party's Leninist role in publishing Connolly's *Workers' Republic* in Glasgow in 1915 and 1916.

James Connolly was, if anything, less of a Leninist than Maclean. But although Vladimir I. Lenin and Leon Trotsky were familiar with the anti-war activities of John Maclean, they simply had not heard of the Irish socialist, James Connolly. As Austen Morgan has argued: 'Connolly remained unknown to Lenin, and his Irish Citizen Army was dismissed as "backward workers . . . [with] their prejudices, their reactionary fantasies, their weaknesses and their errors".'[5] Yet in the 1930s the Anglo-American Trotskyists transformed James Connolly into their patron saint, not John Maclean.[6] Although Nan Milton, Maclean's youngest daughter, belonged to the Trotskyist Militant Labour League in Glasgow in the 1930s, the British Trotskyists did not discover John Maclean until the early 1930s. Immobilised by their inability to understand the Scottish national question, the American Trotskyists still have not discovered the Clydeside socialist, John Maclean.

I

In 1916 there were two factors behind the Second International socialists' bewildered response to the Easter Rising in Dublin. In the first place, the distinctive militant socialist role of the

Easter Rising and Clydeside Socialism

Irish immigrants in Scotland was relatively unknown.[7] Secondly, most of the leading socialists in the Second International (already vaguely aware of the Irish socialists' weakness during the Labour War in Dublin in 1913) did not approve of utilising nationalism as a weapon in the workers' struggle for emancipation.

Inside canny Scotland the Irish immigrants had made a significant contribution to the workers' movement and the growth of socialist sentiments. Moreover, although the Irish immigrants had been marginalised economically as a part of the Scottish working class, they had retained and developed a strong cultural cohesion. This gave them a greater potential to become socialists or revolutionary nationalists than the indigenous Scottish workers.

Yet despite the Irish immigrants' cultural cohesion as outsiders inside a Presbyterian country, members of the Scottish branches of the Irish National League repeatedly clashed over the issue of Irish nationalism versus British socialism. Contrary to Bernard Ransom's assertion that James Connolly did not become an Irish nationalist until *after* he went to live in Dublin in 1896, Connolly's nationalism was already highly developed and articulate.[8] What was of much greater interest than the conflict between Connolly and the Irish National League in Edinburgh in 1896 was his formative antipathy towards Scottish nationalism.[9]

James Connolly and John Maclean never met; but Maclean could not escape the presence of the Irish immigrants in Scotland. When he undertook a speaking-cum-agitational tour of Ireland in 1907, Maclean visited Belfast and assisted James Larkin during an important strike of the oppressed Belfast dockers. This visit to Ireland gave Maclean some leeway in the Irish immigrants' communities in pre-war Scotland.

Before the emergence of John Maclean, James Connolly had focused on the dimension of Irish nationalistic sentiment as a weapon in the struggle between Labour and Capital. In 1896 he had already written to Henry Kuhm, the secretary of the Socialist Labour Party, in New York to direct the attention of the American De Leonists to the problem of recruiting Irish workers in America:

We recognise the enormous importance of being duly represented among our countrymen in America, and we also hope you will perceive how much it would help you, to assist the socialist movement in Ireland. Irishmen are largely influenced by sentiment and tradition, and therefore a word from what they affectionately term the 'auld sod' will far outweigh any amount of reasoning applied to American issues only. Show them that socialism has a definite message from Ireland and you will awaken their sympathy immediately.[10]

In an implicit challenge to the Marxist orthodoxy that 'the workers had no country', Connolly appreciated the importance of utilising cultural factors in the struggle for socialism.

In a retrospective account of an encounter with James Connolly during their shared agitation for the Socialist Labour Party in Scotland in 1903, Tom Bell wrote:

I remember challenging him one day, after a meeting at Falkirk Cross when the question was hotly debated by some Orangemen who were in the crowd, and asking him how he could reconcile being a Catholic and an exponent of the materialist conception of history. His reply was that in Dublin the children who go to Catholic schools invariably turn out to be rebels but if they are brought up in the Presbyterian Church they turn out to be howling jingoes. To me this was not a convincing argument, but it was left at that.[11]

In a later version of the same story, Tom Bell said that the Connolly who denounced the Catholic Church also stressed his own Catholicism. Furthermore, Connolly 'related stories of workers in the Irish Socialist Republican Party going to mass of a morning and delivering the *Irish Worker* at houses on the road'.[12]

By 1907, when John Maclean and James Larkin met and formed a firm friendship, Connolly was working as a socialist agitator and lecturer in America. But just as such Irish immigrants and Scots-Irish as Arthur MacManus joined the Scottish branches of the Socialist Labour Party, so did others like Patrick MacGill join the Scottish branches of the Social Democratic Federation. Though he played a crucial role in getting MacGill's first book, *Gleanings from the Scrap Book of a Navvy*, published, John

Maclean regarded Ireland as a very backward country from a socialist standpoint. In a sympathetic review in the Scottish socialist newspaper, *Forward*, he praised MacGill's particular achievement in impossible circumstances. In a significant sentence, Maclean said 'And to this add that he is an "exile of Erin", meagrely educated in the more or less stifling atmosphere of Catholicism and you have a faint idea of the disabilities under which MacGill has been labouring in bringing forth his first fruit'.[13] Then in 1912 Maclean antagonised John Wheatley at a meeting of the Catholic Socialist Society in Glasgow by insisting on speaking about the materialist conception of history to a Catholic audience. He was, according to Harry McShane, 'opposed to the Catholic Church in a Calvinist way as well as in a Marxist way'.[14]

But just as Maclean retained strong Calvinistic attitudes, so did Connolly remain a life-long Catholic.[15] Moreover, during his sojourn in America and during his trips to Scotland before the outbreak of the First World War, Connolly resented criticisms of the Catholic Church articulated inside the American and Scottish workers' movements.[16] Disillusioned with the sectarianism he experienced in the American labour movement – in the Industrial Workers of the World as much as in the De Leonist Socialist Labour Party – he began to work for and identify with the British Labour Party.

During the vicissitudes of the last two years of his life, James Connolly did not abandon his decades-old hatred of capitalistic militarism. Although he had moved away from the sectarianism of the De Leonists, the Second International's apparent capitulation to the imperialistic war in 1914 caused the so-called 'Irish Lenin' great anguish. Writing in *Forward* in August 1914, he asked: 'What then becomes of all our resolutions; all our protests of fraternization; all our threats of general strikes; all our carefully built machinery of inter-nationalism; all our hopes for the future?'[17] In a series of anguished cries in articles published in 1914 and 1915, he did not attempt to conceal his pessimistic disappointment in the capitulation of organised labour to the forces of militaristic imperialism.

The deepening sense of disillusionment with the timidity of organised labour began in 1913, not 1914. As Desmond Ryan noted: 'The subsequent failure of the British labour movement to back the Dublin workers by industrial action sadly disillusioned him'.[18] A similar point was made by his old Irish teacher, John Leslie, in Edinburgh:

> In the most recent conversation that I had with him, one could note a growing Irishness which, while it might not mean a narrowing of vision, yet showed plainly that if he had influenced Sinn Fein, the influence had been mutual and reciprocal, and that Sinn Fein had made its mark on him; but that does not explain everything. I will venture my own opinion for what it is worth. I have reason to believe that Connolly did not place a very high estimate upon the Labour or socialist movement here. Knowing the man, I say it is possible that, despairing of effective assistance from that quarter, and indeed believing that it would act as a drag upon his efforts to form an Irish Socialist Party, he determined at all costs to identify or to indissolubly link the cause of Irish labour with the most extreme Irish nationalism, and to seal that bond of union with his blood if necessary.[19]

Writing in *Forward* in August 1914, Connolly suggested that 'a great continental uprising of the working class would stop the war'. But although it never occurred to the so-called 'Irish Lenin' to advocate 'revolutionary defeatism' in August 1914, he was within six months of the outbreak of the holocaust of the European war contemplating the possibility of a nationalist war as an *alternative* to the destruction of the socialist proletariat. In a comment foreshadowing what he would attempt to contribute towards in April 1916, Connolly informed the readers of the American monthly magazine, the *International Socialist Review*, in March 1915 that:

> I believe the war could have been prevented by the socialists; as it was not prevented and as the issues are knit, I want to see England beaten so thoroughly that the commerce of the seas will henceforth be free to all nations – to the smallest equally with the greatest.[20]

With a romantic and cavalier indifference towards the problem of evidence, Raymond Ross asserted that James Connolly and John Maclean were committed to the Leninist policy of turning 'the imperialist war into a civil war' inside Dublin and Glasgow. In presenting poetic myths as labour history, Ross did not exhibit any respect for historical fact or accuracy when he wrote that:

> The Easter Rising certainly encouraged Lenin's own immediate revolutionary aspirations as it did Liebknecht's in Germany; but the closest tactical, practical, and political links were with Scotland. . . . Although Maclean was in prison when the actual Rising took place, his agitation during the winter of 1915/16 supported Connolly's preparations for the Rising. Maclean certainly knew what was intended and his political and clandestine contacts with Dublin *suggest* a wholehearted, if not unconditional, support.[21]

Neither Lenin nor Liebknecht had heard of Connolly;[22] and contacts between Connolly and Maclean were non-existent.

From the outbreak of the First World War, Countess Markievicz and James Connolly were waiting their opportunity to initiate a nationalist-cum-socialist revolt. When the opportunity came in April, 1916, they did not hesitate to confront the might of British imperialism. But in restricting himself to the comment that Irish Labour was 'divided on the issue of the [Easter] Rising' in 1916, R.M. Fox was concealing the important historical fact that most Anglo-American socialists had been hostile to Connolly's nationalist role in the events of 1916. In a statement characterising the hard-Left's response to the Easter Rising, the editor of *The Plebs*, the organ of the movement for independent working-class education in Britain, wrote: 'The tragedy of the revolt from a socialist point of view, is that "romantic nationalism" was so largely the inspiration of it; and that Connolly – the Industrial Unionist, the sane writer and thinker – should have been goaded by circumstances into sharing in it'.[23] He was not, of course, goaded into the Easter Rising. Indeed, Countess Markievicz and James Connolly had decided upon the *efficacy* of a nationalist uprising in August 1914.[24]

The key to Connolly's role in the Easter Rising was his 'social being' in different socialist groups in various countries during the previous decades of his life. Inseparable from this social being was a prolonged experience of poverty and visceral hatred of its causes. At the heart of his socialist internationalism were Irish nationalism, the Gaelic language movement and an ineradicable Catholicism.[25]

Arriving in America in the autumn of 1903, James Connolly lived there until 1910. In those hectic, intense and dramatic years, he worked and quarrelled with Daniel De Leon and the American Socialist Labour Party. Then he joined the Socialist Party of America and the infamous Industrial Workers of the World. Although Connolly produced *Labour in Irish History*, *Socialism Made Easy* and *Labour, Nationality and Religion* during his sojourn in America, he did not free himself from the bitter-sweet taste of poverty. As Carl Reeve and Ann Barton argued: 'He was dogged by poverty most of his life in the United States, often barely managing to feed his family'.[26] In contrast to De Leon, however, he did not accept his grinding, oppressive poverty at all philosophically.[27]

Notwithstanding how well known Connolly was in American socialist circles in 1916, very few American socialist editors or writers were willing to portray him as a socialist martyr. From the standpoint of most American socialists, there was great dubiety about Connolly's status as a socialist martyr. Louis B. Boudin, who was one of the fathers of the left-wing of American socialism before he helped to establish communist groups, refused to see Connolly as a socialist martyr. As he explained:

> Revolutionary movements, like true faith, thrive on the blood of martyrs. But in order to have that effect no suspicion of its having been spilt in the service of Baal must attach to it. Like the blood of the sacrificial lamb it must be pure, and innocent of all contamination influence. The real and surpassing tragedy of the recent Irish revolt lies in the fact that its greatest sacrifices were not made on the altar of Irish Freedom – that is not in a manner that could now or thereafter rebound to the advancement of that cause. The guilt of the Unholy Alliance with German Militarism and Imperialism will rest upon it forever, and prevent the blood of its martyrs for ever bearing the holy fruit of freedom.[28]

Although this assessment was unusually critical, it was quite typical of American socialist responses to the Easter Rising.

While William E. Bohm, the editor of the *International Socialist Review*, paid a warm and unqualified tribute to James Connolly the scholar and the thinker – 'the most difficult trade in the world' – he did not identify with the Easter Rising. Though Connolly was one of 'the few who did really good intellectual work in any age or any class', Bohm concluded his critical assessment by insisting that:

> To all such as James Connolly stands as a warning and a guide. Under different circumstances he might have played a part in the world movement like that of Keir Hardie or Bebel. As things are he goes down fighting in a heroically foolhardy skirmish. He wrote one book which proves that a hod-carrier can be a scholar. His name stands as an eternal rebuke to all of us who are blatant and loud rather than serious and true.[29]

The *American Socialist* supported the Easter Rising in 1916; and in May 1916 James Larkin raised the question of the imprisonment of the Clydeside socialist, John Maclean.[30] At the same time Cornelius Le Lone disagreed with socialists like Louis Boudin and William Bohm when he said:

> Only once in a generation is an opportunity like the present afforded to reach the Irish element in America with the message of socialism. That opportunity has been provided by the Irish revolution and the battle of Dublin. This was the culmination of the labour revolt in Ireland which had been in process of development in that country for some years, and the Citizen Army of Ireland which fought in that battle was the military expression of the Irish labour and socialist movement.[31]

In a warm expression of sympathy with the Irish revolutionaries, the *New York Call* asserted that Connolly was 'a Catholic and a North of Ireland man' who had gone to Dublin to 'taken charge of Liberty hall during the absence of James Larkin'.[32]

A minority of socialists in America were sympathetic towards the Easter Rising from the very beginning; and in May 1916 James Oneal published an article in the *New York Call* titled 'How Will the Irish Workers Answer?'[33] But the fiery, class-struggle, internationalist organ of militant American socialism, the *International Socialist Review*, could not regard the Easter

Rising as a socialist revolt. In portraying the Easter Rising as an utter tragedy for Irish socialism, William Bohm said: 'Boatloads of Irish were sent to England. Seven of the leaders were shot. Others were sentenced to long terms of penal servitude. The whole thing was over in a week and Ireland seemed worse off than ever'.[34]

Unlike John Maclean, whose support for the Easter Rising was somewhat belated, James Larkin identified with Connolly and the Nationalist revolt from the very beginning. In publishing the apparently short-lived American edition of the *Irish Worker* in Chicago from January 1917, Larkin attempted to put the question of Irish socialism onto the American workers' map. In an article published on 10 February, 1917, titled 'An Appeal from Ireland', he wrote:

> The Irish rebellion was brought to birth by men and women who had given service to the working class in all parts of the globe. It was not anti-British or pro-German, it was pro-human, and above and beyond all else the real organisers, the men and women who understood the realities behind the struggle, were convinced socialists. Admitting that we were identified to some extent with a section of our people, whose protest was more of an emotional, spiritual and nationalistic character, the basis of the movement was primarily against this despotism of imperialism and militaristic slavery, the natural outcome of the capitalist system.[35]

But although Larkin had not forgotten his old friend John Maclean with whom he had formed a close relationship in 1907, he did not attempt to link the names of Connolly and Maclean in a socialist pantheon during or after 1916. Nevertheless in the American edition of the *Irish Worker* on 10 March 1917, the anonymous author of the 'Glasgow Catholic Socialist Notes' informed the American Left that:

> Mr Harry Hopkins roused our meeting to some tune on Sunday night last. His withering scalding of the labor leaders of today who are traitors to the working class (and the little budding traitors of tomorrow) seemed quite up our street. A work of praise for John Maclean brought forth a great wave of applause, which could

it have penetrated prison walls, would have done John's rebel heart good.[36]

With close links with James Larkin as well as Francis Sheehy Skeffington, the *New York Call* was the only socialist publication in America committed to the Irish cause from late 1916. In May, 1916, its editor carried the following report in the daily organ of the Socialist Party of America:

> One of the first steps taken by Asquith upon his arrival in the Irish capital was to urge upon the commander of the British forces a speedy investigation into the execution of F. Sheehy Skeffington, editor of the Irish Citizen. Skeffington was shot without a trial and his case has done much to kindle anew the smouldering discontent throughout the United Kingdom.

Towards the end of 1916 Larkin formed 'the Four Winds Fellowship' in New York. In reporting the fate of fifty refugees from Ireland, Scotland and England – men driven into exile because of their pacifist and anti-militarist propaganda activities inside imperialist Britain – he focused on what had happened on Red Clydeside in 1915.[37] The brutal murder of Francis Sheehy Skeffington in 1916, a socialist who had been the *New York Call*'s Irish correspondent, played a crucial role in motivating the American-Irish in the labour movement to campaign against British atrocities in Ireland.

II

Walter Kendall's assertion that the De Leonists in Glasgow were involved in the preparation for the Easter Rising rested on an utterly uncritical reading of what Tom Bell published in 1937 and 1941. When he published his book, *The British Communist Party: A Short History*, Bell said: 'The Government suppressed his [Connolly's] paper the *Irish Worker* in December 1914. It reappeared again in May 1915, as the *Workers' Republic*, being printed by the Socialist Labour Party in Glasgow and smuggled into Dublin. It continued to appear until the Easter Rising in

1916'. Then, when he published his autobiography, *Pioneering Days*, without any respect for his own previous dates, Bell said: 'The *Irish Worker* had been suppressed in 1915, and during Connolly's visit to Glasgow we undertook to print it on our machine in Renfrew Street'.[38]

In any event, during the very brief period when Walter Bell and Arthur McManus printed a few issues of the *Worker*, it was subject to censorship by the Government. As R.M. Fox explained:

> After the suppression of the *Irish Worker* Connolly attempted to fill its place with the *Worker* published by the Socialist Labour Party, his friends of earlier years. But it was difficult to run a paper that was printed abroad when the situation was changing so rapidly. And the police were able to seize his supplies as they came off the boat. He decided to bring a printing press into the basement of Liberty Hall and defy the censorship. So, on 20 May 1915, the first issue of the *Workers' Republic* made its appearance . . . Opponents prophesied that the trade union would suffer through his illegal activities.[39]

When a Free Speech Committee was set up in Glasgow in June 1915, the initiative to agitate for the release of Francis Sheehy Skeffington came from John Maclean, not Tom Bell or Arthur MacManus.[40] If Bell and MacManus had really been so close to Connolly as they claimed much later, they would not have waited for Maclean to raise the question of Skeffington's imprisonment. In the light of the sectarianism they were still exhibiting in 1915 and 1916, they were probably lukewarm towards Skeffington because he was a middle-class pacifist.

With a network of sympathetic Irish readers in Coatbridge, Airdrie, Paisley, Motherwell, Falkirk and the Saltmarket and the Gallowgate in Glasgow, James Connolly reported on the anti-war agitation of the Clydeside socialists before the Easter Rising. Although Willie McGill sold the *Workers' Republic* at the Herald League Shop in George Street, Glasgow, most of the men and women pushing Connolly's newspapers in Scottish towns and cities were often more nationalistic than socialistic.[41] But although James Connolly's contacts in Glasgow and Clydeside were often with left-wing Irish nationalists rather than British socialists, he protested in November 1915 against the arrest and prosecution of 'a Scottish socialist, John Maclean'. In an editorial titled 'Free Speech in Scotland', Connolly wrote:

> In muzzling the working class they mean to destroy trade unionism. The fight against Maclean is a conspiracy against the working class . . . To prevent a tyrannical deed we must prepare for action.[42]

But although they did not know each other personally, they had been reading about each other. In depicting Francis Sheehy Skeffington as one of 'the victims of the Irish movement', Connolly explained that Skeffington had been 'condemned to one year in prison for making an anti-enlistment speech in Beresford Place, Dublin'. Jailed under the infamous Cat and Mouse Act, he had been released after he almost died from a six-day hunger strike.[43] It is also probable that Maclean read the article in Connolly's *Workers' Republic* towards the end of 1915 in which Irish Gaels in Glasgow celebrated the anniversary of the Manchester Martyrs. As Connolly reported: 'Some Glasgow Nationalists had already returned and others were going. Throughout the night the prevailing note was the will to fight and to strike the British Empire in a vital spot'. Nevertheless John Maclean was not committed to the insurrectionary approach of James Connolly.

Despite such reports in the *Workers' Republic*, the Irish immigrants in Scotland were at odds with each other over the Easter Rising. With his typical and unromantic honesty, James Larkin used the pages of the American edition to report that some branches of the Ancient Order of the Hibernians in Airdrie, Coatbridge and elsewhere had opposed the Irish revolt in Dublin. At the beginning of 1917, Larkin reported that the 'Penicuik branch of the Ancient Order of Hibernians at a special meeting on 30 April 1916 deplored the outbreak of the Sinn Feiners in Dublin and considers them the real menace to Irish liberty'.[44]

A major factor in galvanising Irish nationalism after the Easter Rising in the American and Scottish labour movement was the brutality of the British army in Ireland. In exposing British atrocities during her prolonged trip to America, Mrs Hanna Skeffington informed Americans about what Captain Colthurst considered to be his 'divine mission in slaying Sheehy Skeffington'. In addressing a large workers' meeting in Chicago, she said: 'I want to say a few words about the psychology of Captain Colthurst. He belongs to a planter family in Ireland – Cromwellian settlers brought up in the tradition of rabid hatred of anything Irish'.[45]

In attempting to turn John Maclean into a 'culture hero' both Raymond Ross and Josef Raszkowski have to ignore Maclean's intense dislike of Irish Ireland.[46] It was, however, manifested in his very sympathetic review of Patrick MacGill's first book. Similarly, it was seen in Maclean's campaign against Catholic Spain after the judicial murder of Francisco Ferrer, the Spanish educationalist, in 1909; and the Sinn Fein leaders of the Easter Rising had approved of the execution of Ferrer when Maclean was campaigning against the Spanish ruling class.[47]

Unlike James Connolly or John Carstairs Matheson, one of the few Marxists in Scotland before 1916 who supported the agitation for Irish independence, John Maclean was not a great thinker. It took the outbreak and escalation of the First World War to free him from the encrustations of his Calvinist upbringing concerning Irish (Catholic) Ireland. He did not produce any significant literary criticism; and before 1916 he had much less sympathy for Connolly's nationalism than Matheson.

In an uninformed, un-historic and romantic critique of my book, *The Rousing of the Scottish Working Class*, Raymond Ross tried to present John Maclean, the 'culture hero' of the bourgeois nationalists grouped around *Cencrastus*, as a very cultured theoretician. By putting down my carefully considered and carefully crafted assessment of John Maclean's place in Scottish history, he argued thus:

> To begin with Maclean was an MA. As early as 1901 and 1902 he had lectured on 'Shelley' and 'Plato and the Republic' . . . Maclean was widely read and did appreciate the value of literature in education.[48]

Clearly, Ross was confusing skills with culture. John Maclean's higher education was engendered within a narrow utilitarian and very authoritarian milieu in which teachers and lecturers tried to transform all 'why' questions into 'how' questions. Furthermore, university students of economics seldom acquired a broad culture any more than they do today. In depicting this actual reality, Royden Harrison, the British labour historian, wrote: 'My father, who left school at fifteen, went to Glasgow University after World War One: took the Adam Smith prize in economics; engaged in correspondence with Keynes; was a complete philistine when it came to literature and philosophy'.[49]

Moreover, although John Carstairs Matheson, the dissident De Leonist in Scotland, alienated most of what he depicted as his 'Orange' comrades in the Socialist Labour Party, he alone remained consistently committed to James Connolly's agitation for Irish national independence. But far from supporting the Easter Rising in 1916, he was fighting as a British soldier in the trenches in France.[50]

At his anti-war trial in Edinburgh in 1916, John Maclean, though sympathetic towards militant Irish *Labour*, distanced himself from the Easter Rising.[51] Indeed, when he appeared before a Scottish court for the first time in 1915, he said: 'But I am opposed to the present military system. It was regarding this that I said, "God damn all other armies." Rightly or wrongly I feel conscientiously that this is not the way to settle national disputes'.[52] In criticising him for making anti-militarist speeches in early 1916, the pro-war supporters of H.M. Hyndman, who defended his democratic right to make such speeches, dissociated themselves from Maclean's pacifism.[53] In the pages of *Justice*, Frank H. Edwards wrote: 'We have regarded, and we still regard, John Maclean's ultra-pacifist attitude respecting the war and the circumstances connected with this terrible world-conflict as being thoroughly sincere, but, nevertheless, wrongly conceived and quixotic'.[54] Maclean was not then or in 1918 a Leninist advocate of 'revolutionary defeatism'.

The Clydeside socialists as a whole did not endorse the Irish struggle for national independence before 1918. Indeed, the Left in Britain was out of sympathy with the Rising in 1916. In glancing back to the revolt in Dublin four years later, Sylvia Pankhurst contributed an article to an American socialist magazine in which she said:

Some of those who fought in it have told me that if, after the British army had shelled Dublin, it had simply turned the rebels adrift in O'Connell Street they would have been stoned for having caused the ruin of the city. But by the execution of the leaders of the rebellion and those who have made it were sanctified for the mass of the Dublin people, and above all James Connolly and his writings gained a wide and far-reaching influence.[55]

On Clydeside the cumulative hostility to the Brits' role in Irish Ireland was fed by the crimes of British imperialism.

Towards the close of 1917 the Irish labour movement began to recover from the 'defeat' that it had suffered in 1916. An important landmark in this recovery was the publication of *Irish Opinion* before it changed its name to the *Voice of Labour* in June 1918. Under the editorship of Cathal O'Shannon, a 'young Gael of vitality and power', the *Voice of Labour* was an ultra-nationalist newspaper with socialist leanings.[56]

Although the forces of Irish Labour seemed broken in 1916, *Irish Opinion* and the *Voice of Labour* played an important role in the revival of a revolutionary workers' movement from 1917 onwards. Notwithstanding the commitment to socialist internationalism, *Irish Opinion* assisted the growth of the latent Scottish nationalism of John Maclean and James D. MacDougall. By late 1917, too, there was a gradual awareness in Dublin that Scottish workers were much less imperialistic than their English counterparts. As one contributor to *Irish Opinion* put it: 'A fairly wide experience of the labour movement in that country [England] has convinced me that the aspirations of the Irish race, for an Irish Republic, are not known and consequently not understood in England'.[57]

By early 1918 Cathal O'Shannon began to repudiate the English trade union movement. In appealing to the Irish workers to develop an independent Irish Labour programme, he denounced so-called British democracy, Havelock Wilson, the English trade union leader, and 'the foreign connection' with English trade unions.[58] At the same time, O'Shannon became the major advocate of Bolshevism in Ireland. In articles on 'Litvinoff and Ireland' and 'Irish Bolsheviks and the International', he invented his own myths about so-called

Irish Bolshevism under James Connolly's leadership from 1913 onwards.[59]

At the same time as *Irish Opinion* associated themselves with the imprisoned John Maclean and established links with Red Clydeside, John Leslie was denouncing them in the pages of the pro-war Hyndmanite newspaper *Justice*. In countering Leslie's criticism, *Irish Opinion* attacked him by saying: 'John's active acquaintance with Irish movements ended in the early 1880s, when he hauled down the green flag with the crownless harp and hoisted the Red Flag'. Moreover, in deepening connections between Irish and Scottish working-class movements, O'Shannon sought to claim James Connolly as an Irish Bolshevik.[60]

By March 1918, the editor of *Irish Opinion* could report on the impressive radicalisation of Dublin and Clydeside. In both Dublin and Glasgow the workers' movements had decided that May Day would be celebrated for the first time on the first Sunday in May. In summing up, Cathal O'Shannon wrote: 'Glasgow and Dublin are the two cities in these countries that lead the van in the militant army of Labour, and from them, if from nowhere else, we may expect a bold lead'.[61] In both of those major cities of the increasingly dis-United Kingdom, working men and women were increasingly radicalised by the introduction of conscription in Ireland.

In recovering the lost historical fact that John Maclean began to co-operate with the Hon. R. Erskine of Marr in early 1919, Harry Hanham did not realise that Cathal O'Shannon played a role in bringing the ideas of the two men to public attention through the pages of the *Voice of Labour*.[62] When James D. MacDougall published his article on 'Marxism in Scotland' in *Irish Opinion* at the beginning of May 1918, he did not even mention the Irish question or connections between the left wing of the Scottish and Irish labour movements.[63]

III

But, although John Maclean's conversion to the cause of what he called 'Irish Ireland' did not culminate in a new anti-British imperialist stance before the early months of 1919, it is possible to identify a major landmark which almost certainly influenced his attitude towards Catholic Ireland and the Irish. Pro-Irish sympathies on Clydeside were fed by British atrocities in Ireland, the radicalisation of Labour in Irish Ireland and the Bolshevik colour of the Irish Transport and General Workers' Union and the *Voice of Labour*. By early 1919 large sections of the Scottish workers' movement had been won over to the cause of Irish Republicanism; and John Maclean followed rather than led this development. He was most certainly not a Scottish Lenin, but the voice of an iconoclastic Clydeside socialism.[64]

The year 1919 was a seminal one in the growth of Scottish *Labour*'s support for Irish Republicanism. Under the auspicies of the Scottish executive committee of Sinn Fein, the 'Republican Demonstration' in Glasgow on 16 February 1919, in the St Andrew's Hall, witnessed a new anti-imperialism in the ranks of the Clydeside workers. In reporting this meeting – attended by 5,000 men and women – the *Voice of Labour* asserted:

> We are informed that this meeting has made a remarkable impression on the labour movement in Glasgow. The publication of the Democratic Platform in *Forward* has removed many misconceptions about the social aims of the Irish people. Further intercourse between Ireland and Scotland, between the forces of Labour in particular, and concerted action for common ends, would help the workers of both countries.

John Maclean had become a supporter of Scottish and Irish Republicanism, and the great James Connolly had 'come hame tae the Clyde'.[65]

NOTES

1. Nan Milton, *John Maclean* (London, 1973), pp. 128–31. In several interviews, Harry McShane insisted that John Maclean and James Connolly had never met or even corresponded with each other.
2. John Maclean, *In the Rapids of Revolution* (London, 1978), edited Nan Milton, p. 74.
3. Walter Kendall, *The Revolutionary Movement in Britain, 1900–1921* (London, 1969), p. 373.

Easter Rising and Clydeside Socialism

4. The myth invented by Walter Kendall about the Glaswegian De Leonists' involvement in 'the preliminaries to the Easter Rising on 1916' is repeated in Raymond Challinor, *The Origins of British Bolshevism* (London, 1977), p. 158.

5. Austen Morgan, *James Connolly: A Political Biography* (Manchester, 1988), p. 11 and Austen Morgan, 'James Connolly', *Biographical Dictionary of Marxism* (Westport, Conn., 1986), edited Robert Gorman, pp. 76–78.

6. James D. Young, *Socialism Since 1889: A Biographical History* (London, 1988), p. 66.

7. James D. Young, 'The Irish Immigrants' Contribution to Scottish Socialism, 1880–1926', *Soathar*, No. 13, 1988, pp. 88–98.

8. Bernard Ransom, *Connolly's Marxism* (London, 1980), p. 3.

9. See the chapter titled 'Nationalist and Internationalist' in my biography of *John Maclean, Clydeside Socialist* (Clydeside Press, 1992).

10. James Connolly to Henry Kuhm, 22 May 1896, Box. 13, Folder 4, Socialist Labour Party Archives, MSS, 3A, State Historical Society of Wisconsin, Madison, USA.

11. Tom Bell, 'James Connolly: Some Reminiscences', *Labour Monthly*, April 1937.

12. Tom Bell, *Pioneering Days* (London, 1941), p. 51.

13. John Maclean, 'Gleanings from the Scrap Book of a Navvy', *Forward*, 18 April, 1911.

14. Harry McShane and John Smith, *No Mean Fighter* (London, 1978), p. 36.

15. Young, *Socialism Since 1889: A Biographical History*, op. cit., pp. 65–67.

16. Interview with Harry McShane, 24 March 1986.

17. James Connolly, 'A Continental Revolution', *Forward*, 15 August 1914.

18. W.P. Ryan, *The Irish Labour Movement* (Dublin, 1919), p. 241.

19. John Leslie, 'James Connolly', *Justice*, 18 May 1916.

20. James Connolly, 'Revolutionary and War', *International Socialist Review*, March 1915.

21. Raymond Ross, 'Scotland and the Easter Rising', *Radical Scotland*, June 1986.

22. Feliks Tych, the distinguished Polish historian, was kind enough to search the Polish and German socialist and communist press on my behalf. After a long search, he wrote to say that Rosa Luxemburg and Karl Leibknecht did not seem to know anything at all about either James Connolly or John Maclean. Letter from Feliks Tych to the author, 25 October, 1989.

23. R.M Fox, *James Connolly: The Forerunner* (Tralee, 1946), p. 219 and 'In Memorium James Connolly', *The Plebs*, June 1916.

24. For conflicting accounts of the significance of the Easter Rising from a socialist viewpoint, see T.A. Jackson, *Ireland Her Own* (London, 1946), and F.J. Gould, *Hyndman: Prophet of Socialism* (London, 1928), p. 212.

25. Young, *Socialism Since 1889: A Biographical History*, op. cit., pp. 66–68.

26. Carl Reeve and Ann Barton, *James Connolly and the United States: The Road to Easter 1916* (Atlantic Highland, N.J., 1978), p. xi.
27. L. Glen Seretan, *Daniel De Leon: The Odyssey of an American Marxist* (Cambridge, Mass., 1979), P. 218.
28. Louis L. Boudin, 'The Irish Tragedy', *New Review*, June 1916.
29. William E. Bohm, 'James Connolly', *International Socialist Review*, June 1916.
30. *American Socialist*, 14 May 1916.
31. Cornelius Le Lone, 'The Great Irish Opportunity', ibid., 9 December 1916.
32. 'Dublin Revolt Quelled', *New York Call*, 1 May 1916.
33. James Oneal, 'How Will the Irish Workers Answer?' ibid., 21 May 1916.
34. William E. Bohm, 'The Irish Revolt', *International Socialist Review*, June 1916.
35. Jim Larkin, 'An Appeal from Ireland', *Irish Worker* (Chicago), Vol. 1, No. 4, 10 February 1917.
36. Ibid., Vol. 1, No. 8, 1917.
37. 'Connolly and Last Sinn Fein Chief Shot', 'Larkin Rallies Refugees Here' and '50 Exiles of British Isles form "Four Winds" Fellowship', *New York Call*, 13 May 1916, 17 December and 18 December 1916.
38. Thomas Bell, *The British Communist Party: A Short History* (London, 1937), p. 33 and Thomas Bell, *Pioneering Days* (London, 1941), p. 49.
39. Fox, James Connolly: The Forerunner, op. cit., p. 179.
40. William Rintoul, 'Glasgow Branch Notes', *The Socialist*, July 1915.
41. *Workers' Republic*, 18 September 1915.
42. 'Free Speech in Scotland', ibid, 20 November 1915.
43. 'Glasgow Gaels Will Fight', ibid. 11 December 1915.
44. *Irish Worker* (Chicago), Vol. 1, No. 9, 1917 and Vol. 1, No. 4, 1917.
45. 'Mrs Skeffington in Chicago', ibid., Vol. 1, No. 6, 24 February 1917.
46. Josef Raszkowski, 'Battlepost of the Poor: The Legend of John Maclean', *Cencrastus*, No. 1, 1979.
47. *Justice*, 23 October 1909 and John F. Boyle, *The Irish Rebellion of 1916* (London, 1916), p. 242.
48. Raymond Ross, 'Hugh MacDiarmid and John Maclean', *Cencrastus*, No. 11, 1983 and James D. Young, 'John Maclean's Place in Scottish History', *Bulletin of the Society for the Study of Labour History*, No. 39, 1979.
49. Letter from Royden Harrison to the author, 19 July 1988.
50. Letter from Jane C. Matheson to William O'Brien, 11 November 1916, in the William O'Brien archives, National Library of Ireland, Dublin.
51. For the wider British context of socialist attitudes towards Ireland, see Herman Gorter, 'Ireland: The Achilles' Heel of England', *Workers' Dreadnought*, 8 May 1920.
52. John Maclean, *In the Rapids of Revolution*, edited Nan Milton (London, 1979), p. 83.
53. The pre-trial archive for Maclean's trial in 1916 is rather mysteriously 'missing'. Furthermore, certain archivists in the Scottish Record Office

often seem strangely suspicious of those who want to probe into such material.

54. Frank H. Edwards, 'John Maclean', *Justice*, 20 April 1916.
55. Sylvia Pankhurst, 'Labor and Sinn Fein', *Socialist Review*, April 1920.
56. W.P. Ryan, *The Irish Labour Movement* (London, 1919), p. 250 and p. 256.
57. P. Coates, 'Irish National Aspirations and British Labour', *Irish Opinion*, 29 December 1917.
58. Ibid., 5 January 1918.
59. 'Litvinoff and Ireland' and 'Irish Bolsheviks and the International', Ibid., 26 January 1918 and 9 February 1918.
60. 'A Falling Star', Ibid., 28 March 1918.
61. 'Connolly's Plan like the Bolshevik program', *The Call*, 18 April 1918.
62. Harry Hanham, *Scottish Nationalism* (London, 1969), pp. 138–140.
63. James D. MacDougall, 'Marxism in Scotland', *Irish Opinion*, 4 May 1918.
64. See my forthcoming article on 'John Maclean, James Connolly and Jim Larkin: The Easter Rising and the Anglo-American Left' in *Saothar*.
65. In the best tradition of the historian in his/her role as a detective, my frequent conversations with Harry McShane and his insistence that Maclean and Connolly never met led me to the archives in Dublin and New York. I wish to thank the librarians in the National Library of Ireland and in the Tamiment Institute, New York, for their practical demonstrations that they were spirituous as well as spiritually on the side of John Maclean, James Connolly and Jim Larkin.

CHAPTER 9

Mobilising the Unemployed: The National Unemployed Workers' Movement in the West of Scotland

George Rawlinson

The organisation and struggles of the unemployed in the inter-war years have attracted much attention from labour historians. Hayburn, Croucher and Kingsford have debated the role and impact of the dominant organisation on the scene, the National Unemployed Workers' Movement (NUWM), drawing on the writings and memoirs of participants like Harry McShane, Sid Elias and Wal Hannington.[1] One of the main areas of political work for Harry McShane during the bitter, hungry 1920s and 1930s was with the unemployed, primarily, though not exclusively, with the NUWM. The history of the NUWM in Scotland is inextricably linked with the social, political and economic issues that affected the working class throughout the second quarter of the twentieth century. The organisation was formed out of the demobilised sailors' and soldiers' associations of 1918. It campaigned on a bewildering array of issues; supporting the struggles of the employed against wage cuts, speed-ups and underemployment; it was active in rent strikes, campaigns against evictions, task work and labour camps, the transference of labour, and discrimination against women workers; it agitated against the means test; defended the Spanish Republic; opposed intervention in the Soviet Union in the early 1920s; fought for peace in the 1930s. From its inception the basis of support for the NUWM lay within working-class communitities and its history epitomises the concept of independent working-class action enshrined in the words of the *Internationale*:

No saviour from on high delivers,
No trust have we in prince or peer.
Our own right hand the chains must sever:
Chains of hatred and grief and fear.

This chapter focuses on the early 1930s – difficult years for the left in Britain – and investigates local activity and the day-to-day work of the ordinary members of the NUWM in three areas within the west of Scotland – Paisley (Renfrew), the Vale of Leven (Dumbarton) and Glasgow. Paisley sheds insights into relations between the NUWM and the orthodox, official labour movement. The Vale of Leven provides a revealing example of the NUWM acting both inside and outside the local political structures. Glasgow, at the hub of local government, was where the struggles of the unemployed were brought into sharpest focus. In the course of the discussion three questions raised in the general literature will be addressed. Firstly, was the NUWM confined to the centres of male employment and the most depressed communities on the Clyde, or did it have a much broader base? Secondly, what was the relationship between the NUWM in West Scotland and the official labour and trade union movement? Finally, how did the authorities attempt to neutralise the activities of the NUWM in the Clydeside region?

Paisley

Paisley was described in 1932 as a river port of some 85,000 inhabitants with a manufacturing base incorporating a specialised local staple in the production of sewing thread. The decline of the textile industry in face of fierce overseas competition and rising tariff barriers sent reverberations throughout the town, precipitating unprecedented levels of unemployment and underemployment. The NUWM built up a solid base in the town in the 1920s and NUWM branches were also well organised within the neighbouring communities of Greenock, Port Glasgow, Thornliebank and Busby.

The developments within the labour movement in Paisley in the early 1930s show very clearly the conflicts and antagonisms that the British Communist Party's Comintern-inspired 'left turn' produced. As was the case in many towns in this period the Labour Party and the trade unions were worried that the unemployed were under the influence of the Communist Party and that they were being drawn away from the official labour movement. In response, attempts were made to set up unemployed associations under the control of the trades councils. These initiatives – too little too late – proved to be of little significance within Scotland, where indifference towards the unemployed prevailed within the Labour Party and most unions. Only four of the sixty-three Scottish Trades Councils ultimately set up their own unemployed associations – Aberdeen, Bo'ness, Dunfermline and Perth.[2]

The activities of the Paisley Trades Council on this question are extremely revealing. In 1930 some members attempted to 'get a nucleus formed, to form a committee of unemployed'.[3] Others favoured developing links with the NUWM. A public meeting was arranged in June, at which Welsh, the Paisley MP, spoke, supported by McKinley, the MP for Partick. Welsh, in response to criticism that he had failed to champion the unemployed, argued that he refused to address 'any body other than that which sponsored his election'.[4] The meeting was very poorly attended. The local daily paper attributed this to the inclement weather. The secretary of the trades council intimated that this effective boycott of the meeting probably had something to do with the fact that the local branch of the NUWM (claiming a membership of 500) was refused a speaker on the platform.[5] The unemployed association favoured by some within the trades council failed to materialise.

In 1931 another attempt was made to build links between the unemployed and the Paisley Trades Council, and again divisions became apparent between those who broadly supported the NUWM and those who were more tied to the orthodox Labour practices. Following on the political and economic crisis of 1931 a resolution was passed by the trades council calling for a conference of all bodies to discuss, amongst other things, the 'establishment of a connecting link between the unemployed and the council'.[6] The secretary of the council wrote to Elgar at the Scottish Trades Union Congress for information on the possibilities of organising the unemployed. The reply received from Elgar contained a copy of the rules of the Bristol Unemployed Association – the model for TUC approved associations. The council debated the issue, which was resolved with a motion being passed by 11 votes to 6 that called for no action to be taken on the matter. A proposal by the minority that a joint meeting be sought with the NUWM was also defeated.[7] A subsequent special meeting did, however, pass a resolution recommending that the Labour Party alter its constitution to allow the affiliation of the unemployed associations. Whether anything came of this is not known.[8]

At the local level attitudes towards the NUWM were somewhat inconsistent. In May 1932, for example, the Paisley Trades Council took no action on an appeal from the NUWM for financial assistance to send a delegate to a London conference.[9] Rather than join forces with, or even support, the organised unemployed, the trades council and the Labour Party found ways of raising the issues of unemployment and the means test which excluded the NUWM. In July 1932, when the NUWM requested that a trades council delegate join a deputation to meet the local town council on the means test issue, the trades council refused, preferring to send its own letter of protest.[10] Yet in September of the same year the trades council executive recommended a £1 donation to a conference on the means test after receiving an appeal from a United Front committee.[11] Such inconsistencies appear to be quite common during this period and show the range of attitudes at the time, as well as the existence of pockets of support for the NUWM within the 'official' labour movement structures in West Scotland.

The high profile of the NUWM on Clydeside, and elsewhere, and the swelling of support for the organisation over 1930–32 stirred the labour establishment into action. No doubt fearful that the NUWM were being seen as more representative of the interests of the unemployed than the trade union movement, the Scottish Trades Union Congress organised a conference on the theme of unemployment and trade union membership in

Paisley contingent of NUWM hunger marchers, passing through George Square, Glasgow, 1930s (Courtesy of the *Glasgow Herald*).

September 1932.[12] In November, the Paisley Trades Council received from the STUC a copy of model rules for organising the unemployed. These were duly circulated to trade unions and a delegate conference called to discuss the issue in December.[13] A month later the Trades Union Congress requested information on the existence of any clubs which had been set up for the unemployed in the area. They were informed that a 'mutual service club' was currently under consideration in the town and that the local MP and his wife had organised an unemployed sports club.[14] Clearly, some sections of society were concerned to keep the unemployed occupied, off the streets and firmly under control. At the same meeting, the TUC scheme for organising the unemployed was severely criticised and ultimately rejected.[15] The trades council was therefore in a position of opposing, in theory at least, the middle class and scab organisations of the unemployed, while not actively supporting the NUWM. By taking such a neutral, some would say negative position, the Paisley Trades Council effectively abandoned the unemployed.

The established right wing in the labour movement were more concerned to keep communists out of the unions and trades councils than they were about the interests of the unemployed. The real issue surfaced in November 1933 when the Individual Section of the Labour Party raised the following question with the Scottish Labour Party Organiser: 'Whether members of the Council and the Executive who had professed or shown marked communist sympathies and leanings were entitled to be members of the Council'. The reply confirmed that they were not eligible to sit as delegates.[16] In Paisley there were two people accused of sympathy with the CP – Jamieson and Murphy. Both had been active in pressing resolutions through the trades council in support of the activities of the NUWM. The matter appears to have been resolved when both men under scrutiny pledged their allegience to the constitution, programmes and policies of the Labour Party.[17]

The left within the Paisley Trades Council did achieve some transient victories. In the Spring of 1934 deputations from the local NUWM and the May Day Committee were received by the trades council.[18] At the council's annual general meeting it was agreed (by a vote of 16 to 4) to send two delegates to the May Day Committee and to call a special meeting to hear the report of the delegates.[19] However, this decision was overturned at the subsequent meeting of the Council where the vote was 10 to 8 in favour of taking no part in the May Day Committee, on which were members of the Communist Party, the Independent Labour Party and the NUWM.[20] The remonstrations of the textile workers, who supported joint activity with the CP and the United Front Committee, fell on deaf ears. At the same time tighter rules were introduced to scrutinise the credentials of trades council members and ensure that all delegates were individual members of the Labour Party.[21]

The conflict between left and right in the Paisley Trades Council continued into 1935. In January 1935, after a vote was taken, a deputation from the NUWM was heard which called for a conference of local working-class organisations to campaign against the new Unemployment Assistance Board benefit rates. This coordinated campaign was supported in writing by the National Union of Textile Workers, the Amalgamated Engineering Union, No. 2 branch, and the Labour Party Individual Members' section. In the face of such pressure the Trades Council agreed to hold such a conference on 10 February.[22] In another incredible volte face, however, this apparent democratically-arrived-at decision was challenged at the next executive meeting. The trades council secretary was clearly unsympathetic to the organised unemployed and declared himself: 'not prepared to call the conference' because it invited all organisations. The matter was deferred for decision to the next meeting.[23] Having prepared the ground the secretary then dropped his bombshell. He reported having received a letter from Woodburn, the Scottish Secretary of the Labour Party, criticising the joint conference decision, and in response the chair ruled the resolution and the meeting which passed it 'out of order'. The joint campaign planned against the UAB scale was thus unceremoniously scrapped.[24] Thereafter the left were squeezed out or marginalised. In the months that followed the Paisley branch of the National Union of Textile Workers was disaffiliated because they would not 'cease their association' with the United Front and the NUWM. The credentials of the AEU No. 2 branch delegates were challenged and the Brassmakers left the Trades Council.[25] To further consolidate the control of the right, Woodburn, the Scottish Labour Party Secretary, gave the Executive Committee of the Paisley Trades Council a sober lecture on 'organisation and constitution' matters.[26]

Lack of support and even open opposition from most trade unions, trades councils and the Labour Party in Scotland notwithstanding, the NUWM continued to campaign and fight for the rights of the unemployed. This struggle was clearly an unequal one, however, and was met with draconian repression from the police and authorities. In October 1932 the *Paisley Daily Express* reported on what it referred to as the first real incidence of trouble connected with the unemployed in the town. Despite heavy rain a demonstration around 1,000 strong marched to lobby the annual meeting of the second ward. After a deputation of five was admitted to the meeting the press reported: 'Difficulty was experienced in splitting the processionists, and the police were compelled to draw their batons on the malcontents.'[27] After presenting their case in an orderly manner, the five members of the deputation were summarily arrested. The crowd followed to the police station in County Square, where two others were arrested, accused of attempting to hold a meeting. Subsequently all the accused appeared before the police court charged with acting in a disorderly manner, creating a disturbance and breach of the peace. Bail was eventually granted of £30 to six of the accused and £15 to the seventh.[28] £30 would have been equivalent to 40 weeks benefit for a single unemployed man or something in the region of 10 to 15 weeks' wages for a man in full-time employment. When the case came to court the charges against the seven defendants were detailed and included:

> Forcing Ernest Webster, vice-convenor of the Public Assistance Board of the Town Council by threats and intimidation to call a meeting of the committee and with intention, thereafter, to proceed to the house of Mrs Marie Fern, convenor of the committee, at 9 Garthland Place, and forcing her by threats and intimidation to call a meeting of the committee.[29]

They were also charged with riotous behaviour and resisting and assaulting seven police officers. Ultimately, four were discharged (one with an admonition); two received sentences of six weeks, and one man, who admitted three previous convictions, got three months.[30] Such were the disciplinary tactics exploited by the authorities to intimidate supporters and muzzle the protest of the NUWM.

Vale of Leven

The economy of the Vale of Leven collapsed after World War One and, as in many other areas, the main grievance of ex-servicemen was unemployment. Overseas competition had crippled the United Turkey Red Company, a major employer in the area; and the Argyll Motor Company, which during the war had employed 2,000 people, began laying off workers in 1918 and was closed completely by the end of 1919. By mid 1922, the

Alexandria labour exchange recorded the highest percentage of unemployed at any Scottish exchange, and even by the outbreak of war in 1939 more than a quarter of the workforce were unemployed. The devastation that the area suffered is well chronicled by Stuart Macintyre.[31]

The unemployed in the Vale were organised as early as 1919, becoming a branch of the NUWM in 1922. One of the leading figures in the local branch was Hugh McIntyre, who in 1919 was a member of the Socialist Labour Party and later became a foundation member of the CP. McIntyre had been wounded during the war and had seen two of his comrades killed beside him. Like many others, he returned from the war with radical beliefs. McIntyre, Dan O'Hare (a victimised toolmaker), David McKim and Willie McLauglan (a sacked craftsman from the Argyll Motor Works) established a local branch of the CP and were amongst the most active in the Vale NUWM.[32]

The activities of the Vale NUWM resembled those of other areas, with campaigns for higher relief and action against evictions. One of the first unemployed demonstrations, recalled Willie McLauglan, attracted only around 50 people. The speaker, Allan Campbell, and one other participant, were arrested and charged with riotous behavior.[33] Similar demonstrations were held on a regular basis through the 1920s and 1930s, drawing press attention, and, more popular community support. Deputations were also organised by the NUWM to periodically lobby the council in Alexandria. The campaign against evictions was also an important part of NUWM work in the Vale. Commonly, the houses of those threatened with sequestration for non-payment of rent would be packed with people to prevent the bailiffs obtaining access. The appointment of 'street captains' who could quickly mobilise the local community made this tactic particularly effective.

In the early 1920s much of this activity was supported by the local trades council and the Labour Party, and the NUWM had delegates on the Trades and Labour Council. Whilst the Labour Party and the CP did joint work in the region, five communists and four Labour Party representatives were elected to the parish council in Bonhill. As a result of Labour and CP cooperation it was therefore possible to grant major concessions to the local unemployed, albeit for a short time. In the process this brought the council up against the wrath of the Scottish Board of Health and the now familiar threat of surcharge on councillors.[34] Thus a distinctive feature of activity in the Vale was the way that campaigning was taken into the council chamber, with activists operating inside and outside the system. By the late 1920s, however, the forces described in the Paisley section had undermined united action, joint activity atrophied and the moderates increased their influence in the Bonhill parish. By 1928, only one Labour Party member and two communists (McIntyre and O'Hare) remained on the council.

By 1930–31 relations between the Communist Party and the Labour Party in the Vale of Leven had sunk to an all-time low. However, the worsening economic situation precipitated a re-emergence of the organised unemployed, and by May 1931 the Vale's branch of the NUWM claimed 1,300 paying members.[35] Reorganisation of local government in 1930 meant that poor relief was passed on to the county council. Thus in the Vale protests were directed away from the parish and on to the Public Assistance Committee in Dumbarton. In November 1930, for example, 2,000 men and women marched to the labour exchange, protesting at the change of signing-on day. The demonstrators secured a day's money for the unemployed which had been lost through the change – a small but significant victory.[36]

Apart from street demonstrations in the Vale, the NUWM was concerned with the rights of the unemployed in general. Protests were made wherever injustice was done. Appeals were made, for example, to the Vale of Leven School Management Committee to supply boots and clothing to unemployed families. The NUWM represented the unemployed at appeals and Courts of Referees, where they often met with lack of cooperation or outright hostility from the authorities. Both the chairman of Dumbarton Court of Referees and the manager of the labour exchange refused to regard the NUWM as the voice of the unemployed. This kind of attitude prevailed even though in 1931 the Minister of Labour, Margaret Bondfield, wrote to the

Scottish hunger marchers in Edinburgh, 1930s (Courtesy of the *Glasgow Herald*).

Vale NUWM supporting the organisation's claim to officially represent the unemployed.[37]

Social events were also organised, as in August 1931, when the Alexandria branch organised a gala day in Balloch Park. An estimated 4,000 were fed on the day, 1,000 red flags were carried on the demonstration, and sports events were organised. A sign of the dark days ahead was also present, as some of the slogans and placards used on the day highlighted the dangers of war.[38]

Glasgow

In the early 1930s, the Glasgow district of the NUWM was extremely active, with 14 individual branches, not including areas such as Bellshill, Cambuslang, Baillieston and Shotts (which came under the Lanarkshire district), nor Clydebank and Milngavie (Dumbarton). Because of the nature of the

NUWM, and fluctuating levels of unemployment, membership of NUWM branches varied, yet there can be no doubt that the organisation was well supported, particularly in the worst years of the recession in the early 1930s. Moreover the male dominated NUWM could and should have been quicker to bring women into full activity within the organisation. Belatedly, in 1929 a women's department was set up on the initiative of Mrs Youle, a Labour Party delegate to the sixth national conference of the NUWM. The head of the new department was another non-CPGB member, Maud Brown. In the 1930s the organisation went on to attract and involve more women. Many branches created women's sections – Springburn's claimed a membership of 300 women in mid-1930.[39] Women were actively involved in demonstrations and protests against evictions and in 1930 the third national hunger march had the first women's contingent.[40] Female contingents were present on the Scottish marches to Edinburgh in 1930, 1932, 1933 and 1938, and on the 1935 march to Glasgow, as Ian MacDougall has shown.[41] In 1932 women from Glasgow participated in the national hunger march. One commented:

> The reason why I am marching is because of the Means Test. For instance, a friend of mine in Glasgow is working in a steel works and earns 10s a week, and because of this his son, who has the misfortune to be idle, gets nothing from the labour exchange. In addition the housing conditions in Glasgow are so bad they are difficult to describe. Four-storey tenement buildings, with seven for eight single apartments on each floor, which are bug infested and not fit for human beings to live in. I am the mother of two girls and, although not as hard hit as many of my class, I felt it my duty to come on this hunger march in order to help those less fortunate than myself.[42]

McShane argued that because the NUWM was closer to the streets it was closer to the women. Nevertheless sexism undoubtedly persisted within the organisation. During the 1928 march to Edinburgh female involvement along almost the entire route was restricted to reception committees and the provision of food. The delegate of the mainly female juteworkers was also a man. However, genuine efforts were made to break down such barriers

Glasgow contingents of NUWM demonstration, September, 1931, George Square, Glasgow (Courtesy of the *Glasgow Herald*).

and McShane may well have been right in his assertion that 'it was through the unemployed movement that the socialist movement came closest to the women in the twenties and thirties'.[43]

The NUWM also developed a strong base in some unexpected places. In the leafy middle-class suburb of Milngavie where, it was said, 'at least two-thirds of the total population live comfortably in villas or in bungalows', out of 350 unemployed in the town, 300 were in the local branch of the NUWM.[44] In this small, affluent area hardly touched by unemployment the NUWM were attracting the majority of those out of work to its ranks. Perhaps the stark inequalities in wealth within such an area as Milngavie explains the strength of the NUWM there? Certainly the branch chalked up some notable successes. Within a year of its establishment the Milngavie branch had won cases at the Court of Referees to the value of over £200. They raised sufficient money to have a full drum and flute band and played an active role organising social events, including galas for the children of unemployed workers, more often than not with the flute band leading the procession through Milngavie to Mugdock Park.[45]

In the more proletarian areas of Glasgow the NUWM thrived. Its supporters incessantly toiled in the interests of the unemployed, whether involved in high-profile events like the national hunger marches, demonstrations on Glasgow Green, organising against evictions, lobbying councils or representing unemployed claimants. In his biography McShane recalls how, in the early 1930s, the Gorbals Unemployed Workers' Committee would meet almost every morning to plan and coordinate campaigns and to take up the daily round of complaints about benefits. They were busy times – every Wednesday a meeting at the Labour Exchange; regular street meetings in Cleland Street. As McShane testified:

> We were at it morning, noon and night; we fought cases at the Labour Exchange for insured workers and at the Public Assistance Board for the others, as well as organising demonstrations and all our agitational work.[46]

The *Daily Record* of 24 September 1931 reported on what it called the biggest unemployed demonstration in any city since the war. Contingents consisting of 30,000 people from all parts of Glasgow converged on Jail Street and made their way to St Enoch's Square in protest against the cuts in unemployment benefits introduced in the 'economy drive' of the new National Government, led by Ramsay MacDonald. In the square an effigy of Bailie Fletcher was burnt. Fletcher had incensed unemployed Glaswegians by derogatory comments about unemployed deputations, including that they were not 'citizens they could be proud of'.[47] The following Thursday a deputation of the unemployed, backed up by a crowd some 10,000 strong, waited on the Corporation, demanding an official petition of Parliament against the cuts. McShane warned: 'I want to assure you that to receive us and do nothing will not quieten the crowd outside'.[48] Hendry, from the AEU, suggested that there were only two alternatives – 'To maintain a standard of living for the unemployed or else use a machine gun to shoot them down'. Receiving the deputation, as McShane feared, was simply window-dressing in an attempt to defuse what most councillors saw as an ugly situation. One of the few councillors sympathetic to the unemployed said bluntly:

> I protest against the hypocrisy of the majority of the members of this council. They have received the deputation, but they have no intention of doing anything. The unemployed will not forget.[49]

Predictably, the council refused to petition Parliament, fudging the issue by remitting the question of dole cuts to the PAC. The protest demonstration that evening was broken up by police, as the *Daily Record* reported:

> Before the crowd realised what was happening, 15 mounted men, who had come down Saltmarket in sections of four, spread across the wide thoroughfare in one rank and headed for the mass of humanity jammed in the semi-circular space around the gates of the green. Behind the mounted men came the foot police who tackled what the mounted police had left. The crowd scattered in every direction and as they scattered the crash of shattered windows could be heard along Saltmarket.[50]

As in Paisley, the authorities in Glasgow relied on the police and the law courts to discipline and deter unemployed demonstrators. A wave of arrests occurred during the anti-dole cuts demonstrations of Autumn 1931. In February 1932 nine were charged in Kilbirnie with being part of a disorderly mob organised by the NUWM.[51] In May 1932, nine NUWM members appeared in Motherwell Police Court and twelve in Glasgow (including McShane) charged with unlawfully demonstrating. The Glasgow accused were guilty of the heinous crimes of playing musical instruments, carrying banners and placards, and shouting such things as 'join the workers' movement', 'to hell with the means test' and 'down with the capitalist class'.[52] The police kept up surveillance of the NUWM and the CP, using their own special detectives, or 'tecs' as they were known, and also obtained information from anti-communist groups, most notably the Economic League (see Chapter 7). Two 'tecs' were present at a Maryhill NUWM meeting in April 1932. They even subscribed 5d between them as they entered the meeting, presumably to avoid drawing attention to themselves.

The chairman of the meeting accepted a motion that the two be asked to leave the hall. As a democratic organisation an amendment was also moved that they be allowed to stay on the grounds that they might get some education! The motion was carried by 60 votes to 6 and the 'tecs' were duly asked to leave. As they departed one was heard to mutter 'All right. Just you wait'.[53]

In Clydebank, as elsewhere, increasing unemployment and government policies on the means test and economy measures stimulated a dramatic growth in the local branch of the NUWM. Formed in January 1930 with just 20 members the Clydebank NUWM grew within six weeks to a membership of almost 300. By that time the branch had taken 12 cases to the Court of Referees, 10 of which they won. Of the cases referred to the Board of Assessors, all were granted benefit. Another small victory was achieved when an NUWM deputation succeeded in getting the labour exchange to reduce the number of signing on days from four to three.[54] However, NUWM members representing the unemployed were invariably treated very shabbily at the labour exchange and council. While trade-union representatives could sit in the waiting room and were dealt with promptly, the NUWM complained of unnecessary delays and being sent 'round the houses to get to the right room'.[55] Such treatment only helped to build up resentment against the authorities and, to some extent, against the trade-union officials.

Frustration could so easily lead to outbreaks of violence. For example, in Clydebank repeated attempts were made to get a NUWM deputation received by the council and much work was put in to rallying support to that end. Committees were set up in all five wards of the town in May of 1931. The demands put forward to the council included a rise in the relief scale and a more equitable method of allocating burgh jobs.[56] Again, in August 1931 an attempt was made to have a deputation received at the town hall. Following a demonstration in the town, a deputation of eight rushed up to the council rooms, only to find that they were locked. The police were called in to eject the interlopers. In the meantime, protesters who were in the public gallery raised their objections to the proceedings. Again, the police were called to eject them. Outside, the police drew their batons, charged the crowd and arrested a number of people, charging them with incitement to riot. The cause of the protest in the public gallery had been the decision of Provost McKenzie to rule out of order a letter from the unemployed which contained their demands. The fact that McKenzie was an ex-ILP member, and that none of the five labour councillors had objected to the ruling was significant.[57] Such obstructionism typifies the strategy of the official labour movement towards the unemployed in the inter-war years.

One of the most active NUWM branches in Glasgow was based in Springburn, where, according to McShane, the CP was strong within the railway workshops. Indeed, McShane had met and worked with Eddie Carr of Springburn in 1921 on unemployment issues, particularly through the South West District Committee of the unemployed, a body on which Allan Campbell of the Vale of Leven also served.[58] Andrew Sweeney returned wounded from the war, became active in his union, lost his job and found himself blacklisted. He joined the CP and later became a leading figure in the Springburn NUWM along with his wife, Jean, who was the branch treasurer. Andrew Sweeney's daughter recalled:

> The Labour party at that time didn't have much to do with the unemployed. The Labour Party saw themselves as of the organised workers within the trade union movement and that sort of thing. And the Labour Party didn't organise the unemployed at all, whereas the Communist Party realised that these workers had to be organised. There was nowhere that they could fit in, they couldn't be members of the trade union movement because they weren't organised in that. And the Communist party obviously saw this need and they instituted the National Unemployed Workers' Movement, and this was an all-embracing thing.[59]

The scale of poverty and the hardship, deprivation and loss of dignity suffered in communities like Springburn is hard for us to appreciate today. In the winter of 1931, in Springburn, unemployed Tom Cannon, an ex-soldier facing eviction, committed suicide. In his house the only furniture that remained was one table and one chair; all the rest had been burnt in order that Tom could keep warm. The week before his suicide Tom's son left home after being disqualified at the labour exchange. At this point Tom was dependent solely on his income of 10 shillings from the PAC, out of which 8 shillings were for rent. He had three sheriff's notices served on him that week, each of which would cost 6s 8d when he came before the court. Faced with poverty, debt and loneliness, Tom Cannon took the way out that many took before him and many have taken since. This tragedy provided a focus for agitation in Springburn and stimulated support for the work of the NUWM.[60] Perhaps more than any other single event, Tom Cannon's suicide starkly illustrates the importance of support and protest groups like the NUWM during the desperate years of economic recession and mass unemployment on Clydeside between the wars.

Conclusion

A number of points might be drawn out of this brief investigation for final comment. Firstly, the scope and breadth of the NUWM's work in West Scotland, with active women's sections, support from the female-dominated textile union, and a strong base in areas such as Milngavie emphasise the fact that this was not an organisation narrowly based within the centres of traditional male heavy employment. Secondly, the NUWM and the unemployed in general were badly treated by many within the official labour and trade-union movement – though there were exceptions. Thirdly, given the level of opposition from the authorities and the official labour movement it is remarkable that the NUWM retained such a strong and viable organisation and achieved as much as it did for those tragically deprived of the right to work during the interwar depression. This is a great tribute to tireless street activists like Harry McShane, and an indication that whilst unemployment was debilitating, it was possible to rally the people against such obscenities as the means test and cuts in benefits. Between the wars there were no saviours on high to deliver the unemployed from their misery. Those out

1 — Labour Party meets to consider drastic action regarding, Unemployed problem

2 — Adjourned meeting of Labour Party Conference to solve Unemployed problem

3 — Further meeting of Labour Party Conference to solve Unemployed problem

4 — Labour Party calls a Special Conference to solve Unemployed problem

5 — Adjourned meeting of Special Labour Party Conference to solve Unemployed problem

6 — Labour Party calls Extraordinary Conference to solve . . . .

The Labour Party Rescues the Unemployed

Cartoon from *The Communist*, 1921–22 (From Espoir and others, *Communist Cartoons*, 1982).

of work had to rely on their own devices. This is a lesson which many are still learning.

This chapter has not done justice to its topic and clearly much research remains to be done. The forced emigration of thousands of young Scottish miners to Canada in 1928 exploiting the 'not genuinely seeking work' clause is a chapter in Scottish history which has still to be written, as is the role played by the Scottish unemployed in the whole episode of the work camps of the late 1920s and early 1930s. It is hoped that this account will stimulate further research into the rich history of the organised unemployed. One thing is certain, and that is that anyone looking at this aspect of labour history will find that the most effective struggles were the ones which were community based, and that the unemployed between the wars often constituted a community. This is a critical factor in the success of the NUWM in this period. By the same token, the disintegration of a sense of community undermines effective organisation of those out of work today. No longer do unemployed workers queue together at the dole office; no longer do they seek community entertainment; the video and the television have replaced the public meetings and the street committees.[61] In the 1980s and 1990s the unemployed have found themselves fragmented and individualised; the very ideas of community and even society have been under constant attack, and this has made effective organisation, along the lines of the NUWM between the wars, virtually impossible to achieve. We may well ask what lessons have been learnt from the experience of the NUWM? Sadly, the conclusion must be, as far as the organised labour movement is concerned, very few, if any. Let us hope that the saying 'it is never too late to learn' proves, in this instance, to be true.

NOTES

1. P. Kingsford, *The Hunger Marches in Britain, 1920–1940* (1982); R. Croucher, *We Refuse to Starve in Silence* (1987); R. Hayburn, 'The National Unemployed Workers' Movement: A Reappraisal', *International Review of Social History*, XXVIII, Part 3, 1983.
2. A. Tuckett, *The Scottish Trades Union Congress* (1986), p. 243
3. *Paisley Trades Council Minutes* (PTCM), 4 June 1930
4. *Paisley Daily Express*, 14 June 1930
5. *PTCM*, 18 June 1930
6. *Ibid*, 23 Sept 1931
7. *Ibid*, 1 Nov 1931
8. *Ibid*, 2 Dec 1931
9. *Ibid*, 18 May 1932
10. *Ibid*, 6 July 1932
11. *Ibid*, 11 Sept 1932
12. *Ibid*, 14 Sept 1932
13. *Ibid*, 9 Nov 1932
14. *Ibid*, 28 Dec 1932

15. *Ibid.*
16. *Ibid,* 22 Nov 1933
17. *Ibid,* 27 Dec 1933
18. *Ibid,* 28 May 1934
19. *Ibid,* 11 April 1934
20. *Ibid,* 18 April 1934
21. *Ibid,* 25 April 1934; 9 May 1934.
22. *Ibid,* 23 Jan 1935
23. *Ibid,* 29 Jan 1935
24. *Ibid,* 6 Feb 1935
25. *Ibid,* 5 Mar 1935; 13 Mar 1935
26. *Ibid,* 26 Mar 1935
27. *Paisley Daily Express,* 13 October 1932
28. *Ibid,* 15 Oct 1932
29. *Ibid,* 21 Oct 1932
30. *Ibid,* 22 Oct 1932
31. S Macintyre, *Little Moscows* (1980), ch. 4.
32. Taped interview with McIntyre held at the Gallacher Library, STUC.
33. Taped interview with McLauglan held at the Gallacher Library, STUC.
34. For a full discussion see I. Levitt, *Poverty and Welfare in Scotland, 1890–1948,* ch. 6.
35. S. Macintyre, *op. cit.,* p. 100.
36. *The Worker,* 28 Nov 1930
37. *Ibid,* 2 May 1931
38. *Ibid,* 25 July 1931
39. *Ibid,* 27 June 1931
40. P. Kingsford, *op. cit.,* p. 108.
41. I. MacDougall, *Voices from the Hunger Marches, vol. 1* (1990)
42. *The Worker,* 29 October 1932
43. H. McShane and J. Smith, *No Mean Fighter* (1978), p. 131
44. NUWM (Scottish Council), *May Day Special,* 1932.
45. *Ibid.*
46. H. McShane and J. Smith, *op. cit.,* p. 172.
47. *Daily Record,* 24 September 1931. McShane recalled these events – see McShane and Smith, *op. cit.,* p. 175.
48. *Daily Record,* 2 Oct 1931.
49. *Ibid.*
50. *Ibid.* Figures vary for the number of people involved in the events. The *Daily Record* (2 Sept 1931) estimated 50,000 'in Glasgow workless rioting'. W. Hannington argues that nearer 100,000 were demonstrating in Glasgow on 5 Oct 1931 and that there were 150,000 on a night-time march in the city on 9 Oct 1931. See *Unemployed Struggles, 1919–1936* (1979), p. 226.
51. NUWM May Day Special, *op. cit.*
52. *Ibid.*
53. *Ibid.*
54. *The Worker,* 14 Mar 1930. The Clydebank branch claimed a membership of 2,000 in 1931, reported in *The Worker,* 27 June 1931. This conflicts with the assertion of C. Watson who has commented that

the Clydebank NUWM branch never claimed an active membership of more than 600. See J. Hood (compiler), The History of Clydebank (1988), p.72.
55. *The Worker*, 9 May 1931
56. *Ibid*, 16 May 1931
57. *Ibid*, 22 Aug 1931
58. McShane and Smith, *op. cit.*, p. 144.
59. G. Hutchison and M. O'Neill, *The Springburn Experience* (1989). In this book the name of Andrew Sweeney is incorrectly given as Joe Sweeney.
60. *The Worker*, 5 Dec 1931; 12 Dec 1931.
61. See B. Pimlott, 'Unemployment and "the Unemployed" in North East England', *The Political Quarterly*, vol. 56, 1985.